The Antisymmetry of Syntax   Richard S. Kayne

D0556781

The MIT Press
Cambridge, Massachusetts
London, England

Third printing, 1998

© 1994 Massachusetts Institute of Technology

This book was set in Times Roman by Asco Trade Typesetting Ltd., Hong Kong and was printed and bound in the United States of America.

Library of Congress Cataloging-in-Publication Data

Kayne, Richard S.
  The antisymmetry of syntax / Richard S. Kayne.
    p.   cm. — (Linguistic inquiry monographs ; 25)
  Includes bibliographical references (p.) and index.
  ISBN 0-262-11194-2. — ISBN 0-262-61107-4 (pbk.)
    1. Grammar, Comparative and general—Syntax. I. Title.
  II. Series.
  P291.K34   1994
  415—dc20   94-26521
                                                                    CIP

The Antisymmetry of Syntax

To Cynthia Munro Pyle

Contents

Series Foreword

We are pleased to present this monograph as the twenty-fifth in the series *Linguistic Inquiry Monographs*. These monographs will present new and original research beyond the scope of the article, and we hope they will benefit our field by bringing to it perspectives that will stimulate further research and insight.

Originally published in limited edition, the *Linguistic Inquiry Monograph* series is now available on a much wider scale. This change is due to the great interest engendered by the series and the needs of a growing readership. The editors wish to thank the readers for their support and welcome suggestions about future directions the series might take.

Samuel Jay Keyser
for the Editorial Board

Preface

It is difficult to attain a restrictive theory of syntax. One way of making progress toward that goal is to restrict the space of available syntactic representations, for example, by imposing a binary branching requirement, as I suggested in earlier work. The present monograph proposes further severe limitations on the range of syntactic representations accessible to the human language faculty.

The primary locus of inquiry is the relation between hierarchical structure and linear order. It is standardly assumed that that relation is a flexible one, that is, that linear order can be associated with hierarchical structure quite freely. A head (H) and its complement (C) can be associated in some languages with the order H–C, in others with the order C–H. There may also be languages in which the order varies depending on the category of the head, for example, H–C when H is N, but C–H when H is V. Furthermore, adjunctions can be either to the left or to the right, again depending sometimes on the particular language, sometimes on the particular construction within a given language.

I will argue in what follows that this picture of the human language faculty is incorrect and that the human language faculty is in fact rigidly inflexible when it comes to the relation between hierarchical structure and linear order. Heads must always precede their associated complement position. Adjunctions must always be to the left, never to the right. That is true of adjunctions to phrases and it is true of adjunctions to heads.

This inflexibility extends to specifiers, too, which I argue to be an instance of adjunction. Hence, specifier positions must invariably appear to the left of their associated head, never to the right.

The implications of this new picture of the human language faculty are widespread. For languages like English, right adjunction has standardly been assumed in the characterization of various constructions. Every one of these constructions must be rethought in a way compatible with the unavailability of right adjunction. The range is substantial: right dislocation, right node raising, relative clause extraposition, comparative and result clause extraposition, heavy NP shift, coordination, multiple complements and multiple adjuncts (here the work of Richard Larson has been extremely important), possessives like *a friend of John's*, partitives, and also relative clauses, which must now be reanalyzed in the spirit of the raising/promotion analysis that dates back to the early seventies.

For languages like Japanese, complement positions can no longer be taken to be to the left of their head. The fact that complements do precede their associated head must be reinterpreted as indicating that in Japanese complements necessarily appear in specifier/adjoined positions that are hierarchically higher than the position of the head. A direct object in Japanese will asymmetrically c-command its verbal head, the object of a postposition will asymmetrically c-command that postposition, and the IP complement of a complementizer will asymmetrically c-command that complementizer.

It is legitimate and necessary to ask why the human language faculty displays the particular linear ordering that it does. Why do heads always precede complements and why do specifiers and adjoined phrases always precede heads? I provide a partial answer to this question, starting from the assumption that there exists a mapping between hierarchical structure and observed linear order that is rigid.

The formulation of this idea that I adopt, in terms of what I call the Linear Correspondence Axiom, has implications beyond those concerning linear order itself. It implies not only that specifiers are an instance of adjunction, but also that no phrase can have more than one other phrase adjoined to it. Similarly for heads: no head can have more than one other head adjoined to it.

The conclusion that adjunction is drastically limited in this way implies in turn that languages like Japanese cannot be uniformly head-final. Of course, the term *head-final* has standardly had a meaning that must now be dropped, since no head can follow its associated complement position. However, the term can conveniently be retained with a different meaning. We can say that a head X^0 is final if its complement comes to precede it (by moving to some higher specifier/adjoined position). In this new sense of the term, Japanese verbs still have the property of being heads that are final. Put another way, Japanese VPs are still head-final, in this altered sense.

Consider now a typical SOV sentence in Japanese. The subject must occupy some specifier position. That specifier position is the specifier position of some head Y^0. However, the complement of Y^0 cannot have moved into its specifier position, since that is filled by the subject, by assumption. Therefore, Y^0 is not final in its phrase.

Strictly speaking, this conclusion is not necessarily valid for Y^0. Perhaps the complement of Y^0 has moved into the specifier position of a different head Z^0 higher than Y^0. But then the complement of Z^0 remains to the right of Z^0, in which case Z^0 is not final. One could pursue this further, but given the finiteness of syntactic representations, the conclusion will clearly be that in every representation, at least one head must be initial, in the sense that its complement must have remained in situ.

Thus, Japanese cannot be uniformly head-final, although it could be that all its visible heads are head-final. (I am actually led below to question even this.) Since by this reasoning no language can be uniformly head-final, the conclusion must be that mixed headedness is by far more common than standard typological descriptions would lead one to believe. (Note that in this new sense of *head-final* English is head-final in certain constructions, too—for example, those involving preposition stranding.) From this perspective, the fact that many languages (e.g., Dutch, Hungarian) are visibly of mixed headedness is to be expected.

The Linear Correspondence Axiom has additional consequences of a different sort. It explains certain basic properties of phrase structure that standard X-bar theory has not, for example, the fact that every phrase must have at least one and at most one head. It does so by in essence attributing certain properties of linear order to hierarchical structure, in effect taking linear order to be of more fundamental importance to the human language faculty than is generally assumed. One of these properties is *antisymmetry*, whence the title of this monograph.

Acknowledgments

Much of the material in chapters 5 through 9 and some of the material in the earlier chapters originated in class lectures during the fall semester of 1991 at the Graduate Center, City University of New York, and at the University of Pennsylvania; it was subsequently presented at the University of California at Santa Cruz and UCLA in March 1992, at the GLOW Colloquium in Lisbon in April 1992, and at the Universities of Geneva and Padua in June 1992. The core ideas of the earlier chapters were presented at the Graduate Center, CUNY, in October 1992, at the New York Academy of Sciences in November 1992, to the CNRS group in Paris led by Hans-Georg Obenauer in December 1992, at the University of Maryland in January 1993 and at MIT in February 1993. More recently parts of the monograph were discussed in classes at the University of Maryland in the fall of 1993 and at the Graduate Center, CUNY, in the fall of 1993 and spring of 1994. I am grateful to members of all those audiences for numerous useful comments and questions, all too few of which I have been able to address here.

An earlier and shorter version of this monograph was circulated in article form in May 1993. I am grateful to Josef Bayer, Hans Bennis, Guglielmo Cinque, Probal Dasgupta, Daniel Everett, Jane Grimshaw, Jan Koster, and Ljiljana Progovac for the helpful comments that they sent me. Again I wish I had been able to take more of them into account.

PART I

Chapter 1

Introduction and Proposal

1.1 Introduction

It is standardly assumed that Universal Grammar (UG) allows a given hierarchical representation to be associated with more than one linear order. For example, postpositional phrases and prepositional phrases are generally taken to be hierarchically identical, differing only in linear order. Similarly, English and Japanese phrases consisting of a verb and its complement are thought of as symmetric to one another, also differing only in linear order.

In this monograph I will propose a restrictive theory of word order and phrase structure that denies this standard assumption. I will argue that phrase structure in fact always completely determines linear order and consequently that if two phrases differ in linear order, they must also differ in hierarchical structure.

More specifically, I will propose that asymmetric c-command invariably maps into linear precedence. I will offer a particular formulation of this simple idea that will yield two major consequences. First, there will follow with few further hypotheses a highly specific theory of word order, essentially that complements must always follow their associated head and that specifiers and adjoined elements must always precede the phrase that they are sister to. I will try to show that this then leads to a series of favorable empirical results.

Second, the requirement that hierarchical structure map uniquely to linear order will turn out to yield a derivation of the essentials of X-bar theory. Put another way, I will argue that X-bar theory is not a primitive component of UG. Rather, X-bar theory in essence expresses a set of antisymmetric properties of phrase structure. This antisymmetry of phrase structure will be seen to be inherited, in effect, from the more basic antisymmetry of linear order.

Let us start from the familiar notion of phrase marker, with the usual distinction between terminal symbols and nonterminal symbols. At least in the PF wing of the grammar, the terminal symbols must be linearly ordered. A linear ordering has three defining properties.

(1) a. It is transitive; that is, xLy & yLz → xLz.
    b. It is total; that is, it must cover all the members of the set: for all distinct x, y, either xLy or yLx.
    c. It is antisymmetric, that is, not(xLy & yLx).

The familiar dominance relation on nonterminals is not a linear ordering. Although it is both transitive and antisymmetric, the dominance relation is not total; that is, there can be two nodes in a given phrase marker such that neither dominates the other.

However, the dominance relation has something significant in common with a linear ordering, beyond being transitive and antisymmetric. Consider a given nonterminal X in a phrase marker, and then consider the set of nonterminals that dominate X. For all X, that set is linearly ordered by the dominance relation, that is, for all X, Y dominates X & Z dominates X → either Y dominates Z or Z dominates Y. Although the dominance relation itself is not total, it becomes total when restricted to the set of nodes dominating a given node. Let us say that it is *locally total*, in this sense.[1] Let us further say that, although the dominance relation is not a linear ordering, it is, by virtue of being locally total, a *locally linear* ordering (in the sense that it becomes linear if one restricts oneself to the local environment of a given node).

The familiar relation of c-command is transitive, but unlike the dominance relation it is not even antisymmetric, since two sister nodes can c-command each other. However, we can add antisymmetry to c-command by simply taking the relation of asymmetric c-command:

(2) X asymmetrically c-commands Y iff X c-commands Y and Y does not c-command X.

This relation is now both transitive and antisymmetric. It is not total, since in a given phrase marker there can be two nodes neither of which (asymmetrically) c-commands the other. But if we restrict ourselves henceforth to binary-branching phrase markers,[2] it is locally total, and hence locally linear, in the same sense as the dominance relation. This is so, since in a binary branching tree, if Y asymmetrically c-commands X and Z (distinct from Y) also asymmetrically c-commands X, then it must be the case that either Y asymmetrically c-commands Z or Z asymmetrically c-commands Y.

We now have two locally linear relations on nonterminals, dominance and asymmetric c-command. The intuition that I would like to pursue is that there should be a very close match between the linear ordering relation on the set of terminals and some comparable relation on nonterminals. By *comparable*, I now mean locally linear. Of the two locally linear relations at issue, it is natural to take asymmetric c-command to be the one that is closely matched to the linear ordering of the set of terminals.

This matching will have to be mediated by the familiar dominance relation that holds between nonterminals and terminals. To keep this relation separate from the above-discussed dominance relation between nonterminals, which I will think of as D, I will refer to the nonterminal-to-terminal dominance relation as d. This relation d is a many-to-many mapping from nonterminals to terminals. For a given nonterminal X, let us call $d(X)$ the set of terminals that X dominates. $d(X)$ can be said to be the "image" under d of X.

Just as we can speak of the image under d of a particular nonterminal, so we can speak of the image under d of an ordered pair of nonterminals $\langle X, Y \rangle$. What we want to say is that the image under d of $\langle X, Y \rangle$ will be based on $d(X)$ and $d(Y)$, specifically by taking the image to be the Cartesian product of $d(X)$ and $d(Y)$. Put somewhat more formally, $d\langle X, Y \rangle$ ($=$ the image under d of $\langle X, Y \rangle$) is the set of ordered pairs $\{\langle a, b \rangle\}$ such that a is a member of $d(X)$ and b is a member of $d(Y)$.

If instead of simply looking at one ordered pair $\langle X, Y \rangle$ and its image, we look at a set of ordered pairs and their images under d, we can introduce the natural notion that the image of a set of ordered pairs is just the set formed by taking the union of the images of each ordered pair in the original set. For example, let S be a set of ordered pairs $\{\langle X_i, Y_i \rangle\}$ for $0 < i < n$. Then $d(S) =$ the union for all i, $0 < i < n$ of $d\langle X_i, Y_i \rangle$.

1.2 Proposal

To express the intuition that asymmetric c-command is closely matched to the linear order of terminals, let us, for a given phrase marker, consider the set A of ordered pairs $\langle X_j, Y_j \rangle$ such that for each j, X_j asymmetrically c-commands Y_j. Let us further take A to be the maximal such set; that is, A contains all pairs of nonterminals such that the first asymmetrically c-commands the second. Then the central proposal I would like to make is the following (for a given phrase marker P, with T the set of terminals and A as just given):

(3) *Linear Correspondence Axiom*
    d(A) is a linear ordering of T.

Chapter 2

Deriving X-Bar Theory

To see how the Linear Correspondence Axiom (LCA) works in practice, let us begin with the simple phrase marker in (1).

(1)

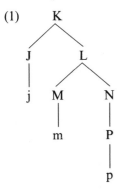

In this phrase marker the pairs that constitute the set A (i.e., the pairs of nonterminal nodes such that the first asymmetrically c-commands the second) are the following: $\langle J, M \rangle$, $\langle J, N \rangle$, $\langle J, P \rangle$, $\langle M, P \rangle$. Since in this simple case J, M, N and P all dominate just one terminal element, $d(A)$ is easy to exhibit fully: namely, $\langle j, m \rangle$, $\langle j, p \rangle$, $\langle m, p \rangle$.[1] These three ordered pairs do constitute a linear ordering of the set $\{j, m, p\}$, given that (1) transitivity holds, (2) antisymmetry is respected, and (3) the ordering is total, in that for every pair of terminals an ordering is specified.

It should be noted that I am crucially taking c-command to be properly defined in terms of "first node up" and not in terms of "first branching node up." Under the latter type of definition the node P in (1) would c-command M, so that M would no longer asymmetrically c-command P, in which case no ordering between the terminals m and p would be specified at all, incorrectly.

The importance of this point can be seen further by considering the phrase marker (2), which is similar to (1) in all respects except that it lacks the node N.

(2)

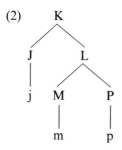

In (2) the set A of pairs such that the first nonterminal asymmetrically c-commands the second is as follows: $\langle J, M \rangle$, $\langle J, P \rangle$. Consequently, $d(A)$ for (2) is composed of the pairs $\langle j, m \rangle$ and $\langle j, p \rangle$. Although the set $d(A)$ consisting of these two pairs of terminals respects both transitivity (vacuously) and antisymmetry, it does not constitute a linear ordering of the set $\{j, m, p\}$, since it specifies no order at all between the two terminals m and p; that is, it fails to be total in the sense of (1b) of chapter 1.

In other words, (2) fails to meet the requirement imposed by the LCA and is therefore not an admissible phrase marker. This has at least two desirable consequences. First, consider whether the complement of a head can itself be a head. The usual assumption, within the context of X-bar theory, is that it cannot be. One could take that to be a basic fact of X-bar theory, but X-bar theory itself clearly provides no account of why it should hold. The LCA given in (3) of chapter 1 does, since having a head whose complement was itself a head would yield precisely the configuration of M, P (and L) in (2), which is inadmissible.

The second desirable consequence related to (2) lies in the even more basic question of why a phrase cannot have more than one head. X-bar theory treats this as a basic fact about phrase structure but does not attempt to provide an explanation for it. The LCA does, since a phrase with two heads would again look like [$_L$ M P] in (2) and would again be excluded. Put another way, the LCA derives both the fact that a head cannot take a complement that is itself a head and the basic X-bar fact that a phrase cannot have two heads.[2]

The exclusion of (2) would not be affected if we added a nonhead sister node to M and P, as in (3).

(3)

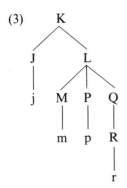

In (3) again neither M nor P asymmetrically c-commands the other (nor are m and p dominated by any other node that is in an asymmetric c-command relation). A for (3) is $\langle J, M \rangle$, $\langle J, P \rangle$, $\langle J, Q \rangle$, $\langle J, R \rangle$, $\langle M, R \rangle$, $\langle P, R \rangle$. $d(A)$ is then $\langle j, m \rangle$, $\langle j, p \rangle$, $\langle j, r \rangle$, $\langle m, r \rangle$, $\langle p, r \rangle$. But again it lacks any pair involving m and p and so does not meet the totality requirement.

From this perspective, (2) and (3) are excluded essentially because the terminals m and p (and the nonterminals M and P that exhaustively dominate them) are in too symmetric a relation to one another. For that reason, they are not "seen" by the relation of asymmetric c-command and so fail to be incorporated into the required linear ordering. Another informal way to put this, reversing the vantage point, is, to say that the LCA, by virtue of requiring d (the dominance relation between nonterminals and terminals) to map A into a linear ordering, has forced the set of nonterminals to inherit the antisymmetry of the linear ordering of the terminals.

If we think of L in (2) as a VP = *see John*, with M = *see*, then the preceding discussion tells us that the complement *John* cannot be dominated (apart from VP and higher nodes) solely by N(oun), as in (4), but must also be dominated by (at least) another node NP, as in (5), in order for the phrase marker to be well formed.

(4) is not an admissible phrase marker, but (5) is (setting aside questions such as the choice between DP and NP). In (4) no linear ordering would be assigned to *see* and *John*. In (5), on the other hand, *see* correctly is ordered with respect to (before) *John*, since V in (5) asymmetrically c-commands N.[3]

Comparing (2) with (1), we see that replacing one of the two symmetric nodes by a more complex substructure breaks the symmetry and renders

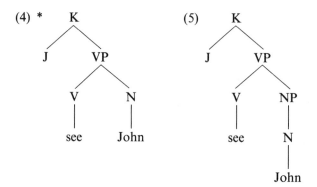

the phrase marker admissible. Now consider the result of adding structure under both M and P in (2), as in (6).

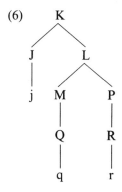

The asymmetric c-command set A for (6) is $\langle J, M \rangle$, $\langle J, Q \rangle$, $\langle J, P \rangle$, $\langle J, R \rangle$, $\langle M, R \rangle$, $\langle P, Q \rangle$. The corresponding $d(A)$ is $\langle j, q \rangle$, $\langle j, r \rangle$, $\langle q, r \rangle$, $\langle r, q \rangle$. ($\langle q, r \rangle$ is in $d(A)$ since $\langle q, r \rangle = d\langle M, R \rangle$; $\langle r, q \rangle$ is in $d(A)$ since $\langle r, q \rangle = d\langle P, Q \rangle$.) This $d(A)$ for (6) is total, but it is not antisymmetric. Therefore, (6) is not an admissible phrase marker.

The problem with (6) is not exactly that M and P are symmetric in that each dominates one other nonterminal. This can be seen by adding more substructure to, for example, P, as in (7).

Concentrating just on the sub–phrase marker whose root node is L, we find that A there is $\langle M, R \rangle$, $\langle M, S \rangle$, $\langle M, T \rangle$, $\langle R, T \rangle$, $\langle P, Q \rangle$. But we now see that the addition of S and T, although resulting in a larger A, has not changed the heart of the problem in (6), which was the cooccurrence in A of $\langle M, R \rangle$ and $\langle P, Q \rangle$, which led to both $\langle q, r \rangle$ and $\langle r, q \rangle$ being in $d(A)$, violating antisymmetry. Exactly the same problem arises in (7).[4]

(7)

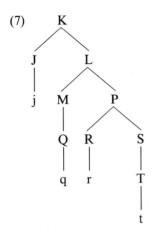

Let us call a nonterminal that dominates no other nonterminal a *head*. A nonterminal that does dominate at least one other nonterminal will be a *nonhead*. Then we can sum up the results of this chapter ((1)–(7)) in the following terms: if two nonterminals are sisters and if one of them is a head and the other a nonhead, the phrase marker is admissible ((1) and (5)). If both are heads, the phrase marker is not admissible ((2), (3), and (4)). If both are nonheads ((6) and (7)), the phrase marker is again not admissible (whether or not the number of nonterminals dominated by each of those two nonheads is the same).

The prohibition against nonhead sisters has one clearly desirable and important consequence, and another consequence that will require a (familiar) refinement of the notion "nonterminal." Let me begin with the first. A basic tenet, perhaps the basic tenet, of X-bar theory is that all phrases must be headed. Thus, X-bar theory disallows a phrasal node immediately dominating two maximal projections and nothing else. X-bar theory does not, however, explain why every phrase must have a head. The LCA does. The reason that a phrasal node cannot dominate two maximal projections (and nothing else) is that if it did, there would be a failure of antisymmetry, exactly as discussed above for (6) and (7).

This explanation for the pervasiveness of heads in syntactic structure has a particularly striking subcase in the realm of coordination. Why is it not possible to have sentences such as these with a coordinate interpretation?

(8) a. *I saw the boy the girl.
    b. *The girl the boy were discussing linguistics.

Again, the answer is straightforward. A phrase such as '[[the boy] [the girl]]' is not adequately antisymmetric and leads to a violation exactly as described for (6) and (7). The required presence of a word like *and* is now understandable: coordinating conjunctions are heads that serve to bring coordinate structures in line with the antisymmetry requirement imposed by the LCA. Consequently, the constituent structure of *the girl and the boy* must be '[the girl [and [the boy]]]'.[5]

PART II

Chapter 3

Adjunction

3.1 Segments and Categories

The preceding discussion appears to rule out sentences such as (1), in which the subject clearly must have a sister constituent that is not a head.

(1) The girl saw John.

Put more generally, specifiers and adjoined phrases appear to have no place in the theory being elaborated here. To allow for specifiers or adjoined phrases, I need to add a refinement to the theory of phrase structure presented so far. I will adopt the notion of segment, that is, the distinction between segment and category that was introduced by May (1985) and adopted by Chomsky (1986a). Let us return to the substructure of (7) from chapter 2, repeated here, that was earlier argued to be inadmissible.

(2)

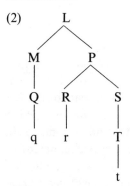

The problem arose with respect to both r and t in their relation to q. Let us look just at r. Since M asymmetrically c-commands R (i.e., A contains $\langle M, R \rangle$), it follows that d(A) contains $\langle q, r \rangle$. But d(A) also contains

⟨r, q⟩ by virtue of P asymmetrically c-commanding Q. As a result, d(A) violates antisymmetry; that is, it fails to be a linear ordering of the terminals.

This result is correct for the case in which M and P are both maximal projections dominated by another node L, and we want to maintain it. At the same time we want to allow for the case in which M is adjoined to P. The segment/category distinction leads to the statement that under adjunction L and P are two segments of one category. The question is how that makes (2) compatible with the LCA.

The solution I would like to propose is to restrict c-command to categories—that is, to say that a segment cannot enter into a c-command relation.

(3) X c-commands Y iff *X and Y are categories* and X excludes[1] Y and every category that dominates X dominates Y.

In this light consider (4), the counterpart of (2) in which L is replaced by P, to indicate clearly the adjunction structure.

(4)

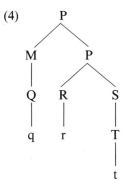

In (2) the problem was that d(A) contained both ⟨q, r⟩ and ⟨r, q⟩, the former as the image of ⟨M, R⟩, the latter as the image of ⟨P, Q⟩. The adjunction structure of (4), combined with the italicized part of (3), has the effect of eliminating ⟨P, Q⟩ from the A of (4), since the lower P is a segment and not a category.[2] Therefore, ⟨r, q⟩ does not belong to the d(A) of (4), and the potential violation of antisymmetry is eliminated.

The A associated with (4) is thus ⟨M, R⟩, ⟨M, S⟩, ⟨M, T⟩, ⟨R, T⟩.[3] The corresponding d(A) is ⟨q, r⟩, ⟨q, t⟩, ⟨r, t⟩, which constitutes a linear ordering of the set of terminals, as desired. We can now think of the segment/category distinction as being forced upon UG by the need to permit specifiers and adjoined phrases.[4]

Unless there turns out to be another natural way to permit specifiers within the theory developed here, the conclusion must be that a specifier is necessarily to be taken as an adjoined phrase, involving crucial use of the segment/category distinction.[5]

Returning to (4), note that what makes it compatible with the LCA is that (the lower) P does not c-command Q, as a result of the phrase added to the definition in (3). Strictly speaking, though, this property of (4) depends only on X in (3) being restricted to categories, the status of Y is not directly relevant. The idea that Y, too, must be a category (and not a segment) does have potential significance. If a segment cannot be c-commanded, and if antecedent government strictly has c-command as a necessary component, then a segment cannot be antecedent-governed and thus cannot be moved. In other words, a phrase that has something adjoined to it cannot be moved out by itself.

This derives the fact that a head to which a clitic (or other element) has adjoined cannot move up in such a way as to strand the clitic.[6] With respect to adjunction to a nonhead, recall that I have been led to analyze specifiers as involving adjunction. We consequently derive the prediction that the sister node of a specifier cannot be moved. This corresponds to a fairly standard assumption.[7]

3.2   Adjunction to a Head

Adjunction to a head, as in the case of a clitic, is illustrated in the phrase marker (5).

(5)

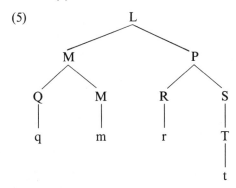

Here Q is adjoined to M. Since M does not dominate Q (only one of its segments does), the fact that M does not dominate R and S is irrelevant to Q's relation to R and S. In other words, the definition (3) of c-command has the effect that Q in (5) (asymmetrically) c-commands both R and S. The A for (5) is therefore $\langle Q, R \rangle$, $\langle Q, S \rangle$, $\langle Q, T \rangle$, $\langle M, R \rangle$, $\langle M, S \rangle$, $\langle M, T \rangle$, $\langle R, T \rangle$. (Note that although P c-commands both M and Q, it does not asymmetrically c-command either one, since M and Q both c-command P.) This yields $d(A) = \langle q, r \rangle$, $\langle q, t \rangle$, $\langle m, r \rangle$, $\langle m, t \rangle$, $\langle r, t \rangle$, which respects transitivity and antisymmetry, but appears to fail the requirement of totality, since no order is yet specified for q relative to m.

Again consider definition (3), repeated here.

(6) X c-commands Y iff *X and Y are categories* and X excludes Y and every category that dominates X dominates Y.

By (6), M in (5) does not c-command Q because it does not exclude it. Q cannot c-command a segment of M alone, by assumption. However, Q in (5) does c-command the category M. This is so because Q excludes M and every category that dominates Q dominates M.[8]

The fact that Q in (5) c-commands, and hence asymmetrically c-commands, M means that the pair $\langle Q, M \rangle$ must be added to A: $\langle Q, R \rangle$, $\langle Q, S \rangle$, $\langle Q, T \rangle$, $\langle M, R \rangle$, $\langle M, S \rangle$, $\langle M, T \rangle$, $\langle R, T \rangle$, $\langle Q, M \rangle$. This results in the addition of $\langle q, m \rangle$ to $d(A)$, yielding $d(A) = \langle q, r \rangle$, $\langle q, t \rangle$, $\langle m, r \rangle$, $\langle m, t \rangle$, $\langle r, t \rangle$, $\langle q, m \rangle$, which is a linear ordering of the set of terminals, as desired.[9]

The fact that Q also asymmetrically c-commands R and S as discussed three paragraphs back is an instance of a more general property of adjoined phrases, namely, that they always c-command "out of" the phrase they are adjoined to. Let us replace Q in (5) by a nonhead, as in (7).

(7)

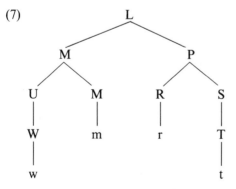

Here, U, a nonhead, has been adjoined to the head M. As before, M does not dominate U, so that U c-commands P and everything dominated by

P. P itself c-commands U, so that U and P enter into no asymmetric c-command relation (as was true for Q and P in (5)).

Now consider W. W does not c-command P, because of the intervening presence of U. Therefore, P asymmetrically c-commands W. Hence, $\langle P, W \rangle$ is in A in (7) and $\langle r, w \rangle$ and $\langle t, w \rangle$ are in d(A). But U asymmetrically c-commands R, S, and T, so that $\langle U, R \rangle$, $\langle U, S \rangle$, and $\langle U, T \rangle$ are also in A, and correspondingly $\langle w, r \rangle$ and $\langle w, t \rangle$ are also in d(A). Thus, d(A) for (7) consists at least of $\langle r, w \rangle$, $\langle t, w \rangle$, $\langle w, r \rangle$, and $\langle w, t \rangle$, which violates antisymmetry, so that d(A) is not a linear ordering and (7) is excluded as a violation of the LCA.

Put another way, we have just derived without stipulation the fact that a nonhead cannot be adjoined to a head, in all probability a correct result.[10]

3.3 Multiple Adjunction: Clitics

The phrase marker (5) represents the case of a clitic (Q) adjoined to a head (M). Now consider what happens if a second clitic (K) is adjoined to the same head (M), as in (8).

(8)

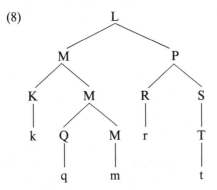

As before, Q c-commands P and everything dominated by P, and K does the same. The problem that arises for (8) instead concerns the relation between K and Q, neither of which is dominated by M. Consequently, K and Q c-command each other; that is, neither asymmetrically c-commands the other. Therefore, no linear order is specified for k and q (neither $\langle k, q \rangle$ nor $\langle q, k \rangle$ is contained in the d(A) of (8)), so that (8) is excluded by the LCA.

What we see here is that two (or more) clitics adjoined to the same head find themselves in too symmetric a relation: both clitics are dominated by segments of the same head and neither is dominated by that head as category. The required antisymmetry does not hold. The conclusion is inescapable: it is not possible to adjoin two (or more) clitics to the same head.

Run-of-the-mill French sentences like (9) appear to pose a problem.

(9) Jean vous   le donnera.
    Jean you$_{DAT}$ it will-give
    'Jean will give it to you.'

However, two other structures are available for multiple clitics, both of which are compatible with the LCA. The one most likely to be appropriate for (9) is (10).

(10)

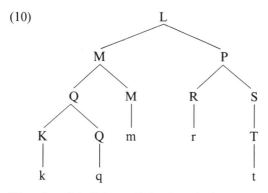

Here the clitic Q has adjoined to the head M, and the clitic K has in turn adjoined to the clitic Q. Q c-commands P and everything P dominates, as before. Since K is not dominated by Q (or by M), K c-commands P and everything P dominates, too. In other words, both K and Q asymmetrically c-command R, S, and T (but not P, since P c-commands both K and Q). The A for (10) is therefore $\langle K, Q \rangle$,[11] $\langle K, M \rangle$, $\langle Q, M \rangle$, $\langle M, R \rangle$, $\langle M, S \rangle$, $\langle M, T \rangle$, $\langle K, R \rangle$, $\langle K, S \rangle$, $\langle K, T \rangle$, $\langle Q, R \rangle$, $\langle Q, S \rangle$, $\langle Q, T \rangle$, $\langle R, T \rangle$. The corresponding d(A) is $\langle k, q \rangle$, $\langle k, m \rangle$, $\langle q, m \rangle$, $\langle m, r \rangle$, $\langle m, t \rangle$, $\langle k, r \rangle$, $\langle k, t \rangle$, $\langle q, r \rangle$, $\langle q, t \rangle$, $\langle r, t \rangle$, which is a linear ordering of the set of terminals, as desired.

The two clitics of (9) could thus be taken to form a constituent '[vous le]',[12] with *vous* adjoined to *le*. From this perspective, clitic ordering and cooccurrence restrictions could be looked at as follows: the impossibility of **Jean le vous donnera* could be due to the impossibility of adjoining another clitic to *vous* (and similarly *nous, me, te, se*)[13] in French.[14] I have no proposal to make concerning the impossibility of expressing the French counterpart to *They will introduce me to him* with two clitics.

(11) a. *Ils   me lui   présenteront.
       they me him$_{DAT}$ will-introduce
     b. *Ils lui me présenteront.

Although (11b) may well be excludable on the grounds suggested above (that *me* cannot be adjoined to), (11a) is unexpected. Of interest, nonetheless, is that for many speakers, the clitic sequence *me lui* is better in (12) than in (11a).[15]

(12) ?Elle me   lui   semble infidèle.
      she me$_{DAT}$ him$_{DAT}$ seems   unfaithful
      'She seems to me unfaithful to him.'

This kind of contrast might be analyzed by attributing to *me lui* in (12) a different constituent structure from that holding in (11a), which probably involves (unsuccessful) adjunction of *me* to *lui*. Although no more than one clitic can be adjoined to a given head, the possibility still remains open that two adjacent clitics are to be analyzed as being adjoined to two distinct (nonclitic) heads. In other words, it might be that *me* in (12) is adjoined to one functional head, and *lui* to the next functional head below that. Whether or not this is correct for (12), it is almost certain to be correct for some instances of adjacent clitics. This amounts to saying that the phenomenon of *split clitics* discussed in Kayne 1991, pp. 660ff., is found not only when the clitics in question are separated by overt material but also, as one would expect, when they are not.[16]

In summary, from the perspective of the LCA, sequences of clitics must not be analyzed as successive adjunctions to the same head but instead should be analyzed as involving either adjunctions to distinct functional heads (e.g., one clitic to Tense, one to Agr) or adjunctions of one clitic to another, or some combination thereof.

3.4 Multiple Adjunctions: Nonheads

The antisymmetry requirement induced by the LCA has the same consequence for adjunctions of nonheads to nonheads as it does for adjunctions of heads to heads, as discussed for clitics in the previous section. The relevant phrase marker has the form shown in (13).

(13)

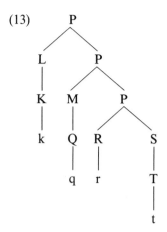

In (13) the nonhead M has been adjoined to the nonhead P, and the nonhead L has been further adjoined to the two-segment category P that was the output of the first adjunction.

In a way partially parallel to the discussion of (8), there is a problem with (13) concerning the relation between k and q. The problem here is specifically that L asymmetrically c-commands Q and at the same time M asymmetrically c-commands K. Thus, $\langle L, Q \rangle$ and $\langle M, K \rangle$ are both in the A of (13), so that $\langle k, q \rangle$ and $\langle q, k \rangle$ are both in d(A), with a consequent violation of antisymmetry.

I conclude that the adjunction of more than one nonhead to a given nonhead is impossible. Since in this theory specifiers are a case of adjunction, we derive the fact (stated by X-bar theory) that a given phrase can have only one specifier.

This limitation on specifiers is not controversial (so that its derivation is clearly desirable), but the more general limitation on adjoined phrases is potentially controversial, since it is usually assumed that more than one phrase can be adjoined to a given projection (nonhead) and also that a phrase can be adjoined to a phrase that already has a specifier.

3.5 Specifiers

Let me begin indirectly by pointing out that the present theory does allow a certain kind of multiple adjunction, parallel to that seen above in the case of clitics. More specifically, it is permissible to adjoin Y to X and Z to Y. The relevant phrase marker looks like (14).

(14)

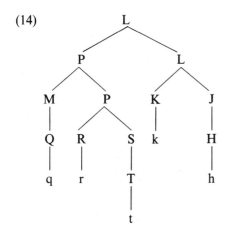

Here, the nonhead P has been adjoined to the nonhead L, and the non-head M has been adjoined to P.

In (14) M is dominated neither by P nor by L. Consequently, M asymmetrically c-commands K, J, and H (see note 3), so that the asymmetric c-command set A contains $\langle M, K \rangle$, $\langle M, J \rangle$, and $\langle M, H \rangle$. Since M dominates q, d(A) contains $\langle q, k \rangle$ and $\langle q, h \rangle$. Similarly for $\langle M, R \rangle$, $\langle M, S \rangle$, $\langle M, T \rangle$ and $\langle q, r \rangle$, $\langle q, t \rangle$; also $\langle R, T \rangle$, $\langle K, H \rangle$ and $\langle r, t \rangle$, $\langle k, h \rangle$. The remaining pairs $\langle r, k \rangle$, $\langle r, h \rangle$, $\langle t, k \rangle$, $\langle t, h \rangle$ come into d(A) by virtue of P asymmetrically c-commanding K and J. (K and J do not c-command P, since L, which dominates K and J, does not dominate P.) (14) is thus compatible with the LCA.

This type of phrase marker takes on particular interest when we recall that in the theory being developed here specifiers are an instance of adjunction. Therefore, M in (14) could just as well be a specifier of P and P a specifier of L—in which case the specifier of the specifier of L would asymmetrically c-command K and J and everything dominated by K and J. Taking L = IP, K = I, and J = VP, we reach the conclusion that the specifier of the subject of IP asymmetrically c-commands I and VP and everything within VP.

This conclusion has some favorable consequences. First, it brings back into the fold the recalcitrant cases of pronoun binding by a quantifier phrase that are discussed by Reinhart (1983, p. 177). For example:

(15) Every girl's father thinks she's a genius.

From the present perspective, the fact that *every girl* is in the specifier of the subject DP does not interfere with its binding the pronoun. Since specifiers are adjoined phrases, the definition of c-command adopted above, and repeated here, has the effect that *every girl* in (15) does in fact c-command *she*.

(16) X c-commands Y iff X and Y are categories and X excludes Y and every category that dominates X dominates Y.

Second, we now have an account of contrasts like the following:

(17)   Nobody's articles ever get published fast enough.

(18)   *Articles by nobody ever get published fast enough.

(19)   *The articles that nobody writes ever get published fast enough.

(20)   Nobody ever gets their articles published fast enough.

The polarity item *ever* needs to be c-commanded by an appropriate licenser, in these examples *nobody*. In agreement with Larson (1988, p. 337), I take c-command of the polarity item by the negative licenser to be a necessary condition for well-formedness. (18) and (19) are excluded because c-command between *nobody* and *ever* does not hold. In the present framework, *nobody* in (17) does c-command *ever*, as desired.

Third, Webelhuth (1992, chap. 4) has argued that pied-piping in (nonecho) interrogatives is licensed only by specifiers (as opposed to modifiers and complements). This is particularly clear in embedded interrogatives, where interference from echo constructions is not at issue. For example:

(21)   We know whose articles those are.

(22)   *We know articles by who(m) those are.

(23)   *I wonder people from what city the game is likely to attract.

This contrast can be partially unified with those discussed in the preceding paragraphs on negative polarity items and pronoun binding as follows. Assume that these (nonecho) interrogatives have a [+wh] head (C^0) that the *wh*-phrase (*who, what city*) must be paired with.[17] Then (21) can be distinguished from (22)–(23) if (24) holds as a necessary condition.

(24) The *wh*-phrase in interrogatives must asymmetrically c-command the [+wh] head.

Taking *who* in (21) to be the specifier of (the highest head of) *whose articles*, it follows from (16) (plus the specifiers-as-adjoined-phrases hypothesis) that *who* in (21) meets (24), whereas the *who(m)* and *what* of (22) and (23) clearly do not.[18]

In (my) colloquial English, the pied-piping of a prepositional phrase in interrogatives (and relatives) is not possible.[19]

(25) a. *We want to know about what you're thinking.
     b. *Tell me at who(m) you were looking.
     c. *Nobody knows to what school he goes.
     d. *I can't figure out for which kid you bought it.
     e. *Tell us from where you got that.

This follows directly from (24) since the complement of a preposition internal to Spec,CP does not c-command C^0.

The many languages that do allow the equivalent of (25) must permit the object of the preposition to move to Spec,PP at LF (cf. Chomsky 1993, p. 35).

(26) ... $[_{CP}[_{PP}$ what$_i$ $[_{PP}$ about $[e_i]]]$ $[_{IP}$ ...

The fact that colloquial English does not itself allow (26), and therefore does not have (25), is presumably to be related to the fact that it does allow preposition stranding. For example:

(27) We want to know what you're thinking about.

One aspect of this relation can be expressed straightforwardly by claiming that the derivation of (27) involves movement of *what* through the specifier of the PP headed by *about*, essentially as proposed by Van Riemsdijk (1978, chap. 6).[20] Thus, both (27) and (25) will involve movement of the *wh*-phrase to Spec,PP, overtly in (27) (with subsequent movement to Spec,CP)[21] and covertly in (25), in those languages that permit (25).

Related to this discussion is the partial acceptability of (the noncolloquial) (28) and (29).

(28) ?The father of every eight-year-old girl$_i$ thinks she$_i$'s a genius.

(29) ?The author of no linguistics article ever wants it to go unread.

These suggest that the object of a postnominal *of* can to some extent be moved to Spec,DP in LF.

If I am correct in arguing that a specifier c-commands out of the phrase that it is the specifier of, then an obvious question arises concerning reflexives. Consider (30).

(30) *Every girl's father admires herself.

One possibility would be to say that in this sentence *every girl* is prevented from being the antecedent of the reflexive since there is a closer potential antecedent, *every girl's father*.[22] However, this would leave unexplained the fact that the sort of pronoun binding found in (15) is not sensitive to a parallel "closest antecedent" requirement, as can be seen in (31).

(31) Every girl's father thinks he knows what's best for her.

Here, *her* can be bound by *every girl* even though *every girl's father* is a potential pronoun binder, as shown in particular by the fact that it can actually bind *he*.

I will instead pursue an approach to (30) based on Szabolcsi's (1981; 1983; 1992) analysis of Hungarian possessives, as transposed to English in Kayne 1993, sect. 2.2. In a number of clear cases the possessor in Hungarian is preceded by an independent D^0, much as in the Italian example (32), with the difference that in Hungarian the prenominal possessor is not limited to being a pronoun.

(32) il   mio libro
      the my book

The crucial step in the transposition to English is to take the English prenominal possessor to likewise be preceded by D^0, which in English must be empty.

(33) $[_{DP} \ldots D^0 [\text{John} [\text{'s book}]]]$

There are now two relevant specifier positions, that associated with the head *'s*, in which *John* is found, and that associated with D^0, which is indicated in (33) by the three dots.

Szabolcsi argues that Spec,D^0 is an operator position. Let us assume that, insofar as the notion "antecedent" is concerned, operator positions, although essential to operator binding of a pronoun qua variable, are invisible to Conditions A, B, and C of the binding theory. Let us further assume that in English the possessor phrase, when an operator phrase, moves up in LF to Spec,D^0. Then the operator binding of the pronoun in (31) and (15) will be legitimate, since Spec,D^0 c-commands out of DP. (Similarly, in (17) *nobody* will c-command the polarity item at LF, and in (21) *who* will c-command C^0 at LF.)

On the other hand, (30) will be excluded, as desired, as follows: From its visible position in Spec,*'s*, the phrase *every girl* does not c-command *herself* (because DP dominates the former without dominating the latter). When *every girl* moves at LF to Spec,D^0, it does come to c-command *herself* (because in its LF position *every girl* is not dominated by DP). But

this c-command relation holds between an operator position and a reflexive, and therefore does not suffice to license the latter, by assumption.

The primary distinction here is thus whether a phrase reaches the
highest specifier within DP. If it does, then it can c-command out of DP,
by virtue of the definition (16) of c-command and the fact that specifier
positions are instances of adjunction. If it does not, then it cannot.
The clear contrast between the following two sentences is accounted for
straightforwardly:

(34) *John considers John's father highly intelligent.

(35) ?John's father considers John highly intelligent.

(34) is a standard Condition C violation. (35) is substantially better because the first instance of *John*, in Spec,'s (not the highest specifier within
DP), does not c-command the second.[23]

(36) does not violate Condition C for a similar reason: the pronoun
does not c-command *John*.

(36) His father considers John highly intelligent.

Nor does *John* c-command *him* in (37), so Condition B is not violated.

(37) John's father considers him highly intelligent.

On the other hand, Loubana Mouchaweh has brought to my attention the
fact that the counterpart of (36) is not possible in (her Damascus) Arabic.[24] From the standard c-command perspective, this apparent Condition C violation in Arabic is unexpected. From the present perspective, it
might be accounted for if pronouns in (the relevant varieties of) Arabic
did have to move to the highest specifier within DP.

3.6 Verb-Second Effects

In the previous section I discussed some issues related to the claim that
specifiers c-command out of their containing category. This property is
due to the union of two factors. The first is that the LCA forces specifiers
to be analyzed as instances of adjunction (otherwise, a specifier and its
sister phrase would be too "symmetric"). The second is the definition
(16) of c-command in terms of category dominance (rather than segment
dominance).

As noted at the end of section 3.4, these two factors have the desirable
effect of limiting the number of specifiers of a given category to one. In

addition, they have the more general effect of limiting a given phrase to having at most one adjoined phrase (including a specifier). If a phrase XP had a specifier YP, and if another phrase ZP were further adjoined to XP, then YP and ZP would c-command each other, leading to a violation of the LCA, as discussed earlier for (13).

This severe limitation on adjunction that the LCA derives surely appears to be too restrictive. I will nonetheless take it to be correct. That it is correct is suggested by the following considerations. First, it may provide a deep account of (at least one aspect of) the well-known obligatory verb-second effect found in the Germanic languages other than English. A German example would be (38).

(38) *Gestern   Peter tanzte.
       yesterday Peter danced

Taking *Peter* to be the specifier of IP, adjunction of *gestern* to IP is immediately prohibited.[25]

For the English sentence parallel to (38), which is grammatical, I am led to propose that a covert functional head above a root IP is available and that *yesterday* can adjoin to its projection.

(39) Yesterday Peter danced.

English actually does display the restriction on adjunction seen in (38).

(40) *Never Peter has danced so well.

If the auxiliary raises to a position above the subject, then the negative phrase can be initial.

(41) Never has Peter danced so well.

I take *never* here to be adjoined to the projection of the functional head that contains *has*. This strategy is not available with *yesterday*.

(42) *Yesterday did Peter dance.

This paradigm suggests that (39) is the covert equivalent of (42) and that the difference between *yesterday* and *never* is that only negative phrases (and phrases with *only*) require that the functional head above IP be overtly filled.[26]

That (39) and (41) are indeed parallel is suggested further by their similar behavior in embedded contexts.

(43) I didn't know *(that) yesterday Peter danced.

(44) I didn't know *(that) never had Peter danced so well.

Without the extra functional head above IP, (43) is prohibited as an instance of double adjunction to the same projection. With that extra head, (43), exactly like (44), is embeddable as a complement introduced by *that*, but not as a complement with no overt complementizer.[27]

Another aspect of obligatory verb-second is seen in (45).

(45) *Peter immer tanzt.

      Peter always dances

In the English equivalent the adverb *always* can presumably be adjoined to a projection below that of the highest I. If so, then the proposal I made for (38) does not carry over to (45), which could instead be thought of as parallel to the French (46), for which the standard account is rather to require the verb to raise to the highest I node (see Emonds 1978; Pollock 1989).

(46) *Pierre toujours danse.

      Pierre always   dances

The idea that (38) and (45) are not entirely the same phenomenon is reinforced by the fact that Icelandic allows the equivalent of (45) with some adverbs (see Thráinsson 1985), but apparently not the equivalent of (38).

My proposal for (39) is best understood in the context of the following more fundamental question: why are there so many functional heads? This question is not particularly bothersome in the case of the interpretively contentful functional heads such as Tense. Tense is present in the overt syntax and at LF, and there are well-known advantages to taking it to be an independent head (see Chomsky 1957). Less obvious is the status of agreement. It is evident from languages like Chinese that overt agreement can be completely dispensed with. At the same time there is evidence for abstract Agr heads (even in Chinese; see Chiu 1991). Chomsky (1993) makes significant use of his generalized Agr_O hypothesis (and, of course, of Agr_S). Belletti (1990) and Cardinaletti and Roberts (1990) have given interesting arguments for a second Agr_S, above and beyond the familiar one. I have found evidence, reported in Kayne 1993, for an abstract Agr_S in participial clauses in Romance. Finally, Sportiche (1992) has argued that an extremely wide variety of phrases must be licensed via a spec-head relation with an appropriate head.

The theory developed here, based on the LCA and the characterization of c-command in terms of categories, provides at least a partial answer to this question. Assuming that phrases of various kinds must move out of their base position at some point in the derivation, the answer is that functional heads make landing sites available. Spec-head configurations are used for licensing for a principled and simple reason: there is no other possibility. Given that double adjunction to the same projection is prohibited,[28] there must, for every moved phrase, be a distinct head to whose projection it can adjoin as specifier.[29]

From this perspective, spec-head licensing can be broken into two parts. One is simply that every maximal projection[30] that is not the complement of some head must be the specifier of some head (since no other phrasal adjunction sites are available) and in that sense can be said to be licensed by the head it is specifier of.

The second aspect of spec-head licensing involves the question of matching/agreement—that is, the question, which I will not systematically pursue in this monograph, of what phrase can be the specifier of what head.[31] I would, however, like to call attention to one aspect of this question. Certain heads are intrinsically contentful, such as lexical heads and functional heads like Tense and Aspect. In some cases a moved phrase will become the specifier of a contentful head. In cases where movement is called for, but where no contentful head is available, the moved phrase must become the specifier of a head lacking intrinsic content. It may be that this is what is meant by Agr^0—namely, that Agr^0 is properly thought of as a label for head positions imposed upon phrase markers by the paucity of available adjunction sites, with this paucity following from the present theory.[32]

3.7   Adjunction of a Head to a Nonhead

Can a head be adjoined to a nonhead? Chomsky (1986a, p. 73) shows that such adjunction followed by further movement back to a head position leads to an undesirable result. I will now show that the desired prohibition follows directly from the theory developed here. In its essentials, the phrase marker that corresponds to Chomsky's case is (47).

P here is the nonhead to which the head M has adjoined. K is the next higher head to which M is to move. (Note that the argument that follows holds independently of where M originates.)

To see that (47) violates the LCA, consider k and m. K c-commands M, but M also c-commands K (since M is not dominated by P). Furthermore, although K c-commands P, P also c-commands K. Therefore, A for (47)

(47)

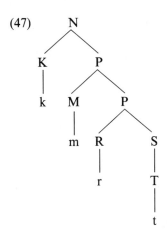

contains no pair that could lead, via the mapping d, to either $\langle k, m \rangle$ or $\langle m, k \rangle$ being in d(A). Thus, d(A) will fail the requirement of totality and hence fail to constitute the necessary linear ordering of the terminals of (47), as desired.[33]

Observe that although k and m yield a violation in (47) (essentially because they are too symmetric to one another), there is no parallel violation based on m and r. M c-commands R in (47), but R does not c-command M (since P dominates R without dominating M). Hence, M asymmetrically c-commands R, leading to $\langle m, r \rangle$ being in d(A), so that m and r pose no totality requirement problem.

This means that (47) without K (and N), as shown in (48), is well formed.

(48)

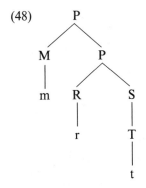

Assume, however, that the highest element of a chain of heads must have a specifier, in the sense of having a phrase that asymmetrically c-commands it within its maximal projection (or within the maximal projection of the head it is adjoined to). Then (48) is not legitimate. Furthermore, adjoining a nonhead to P in (48) would not yield a specifier of M, since M would c-command that adjoined phrase (given that M is not dominated by P). Adjunction of a head to a nonhead is thus systematically unavailable.

Since specifiers are instances of adjunction, it follows that specifiers cannot be heads.[34]

Chapter 4

Word Order

4.1 The Specifier-Complement Asymmetry

I would now like to explore the relation between the LCA, repeated in (1), and the ordering, in terms of precedence/subsequence, of the terminals of a given phrase marker.

(1) *Linear Correspondence Axiom*
$d(A)$ is a linear ordering of T.

Implicit in the earlier discussion was the assumption (not used until now) that the linear ordering of terminals constituted by $d(A)$ must directly and uniformly provide the precedence/subsequence relation for the set of terminals.

However, nothing said so far tells us whether it is precedence itself or rather subsequence that is provided. Put another way, the question is whether asymmetric c-command is mapped (by d) to precedence or to subsequence. If it is to precedence, then the following holds:

(2) Let X, Y be nonterminals and x, y terminals such that X dominates x and Y dominates y. Then if X asymmetrically c-commands Y, x precedes y.

Were asymmetric c-command to map to subsequence, then *precedes* in (2) would have to be replaced by *follows*. I will proceed to argue that (2) is true as stated, namely, that asymmetric c-command does map to precedence.

Let us temporarily hold the choice between precedence and subsequence in abeyance, however, and consider again a phrase marker representing a head with complement and specifier, as in (3).

(3)

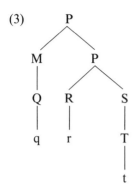

Since M asymmetrically c-commands R (the head)—that is, A contains $\langle M, R \rangle$—it follows that d(A) contains $\langle q, r \rangle$. Similarly, since R asymmetrically c-commands T, d(A) contains $\langle r, t \rangle$. It therefore follows that with respect to the ordering of terminals, q and t are necessarily on opposite sides of the head r.

A similar conclusion would hold if M dominated a more complex phrase than just Q and if S dominated a more complex phrase than just T, as in (4).

(4)

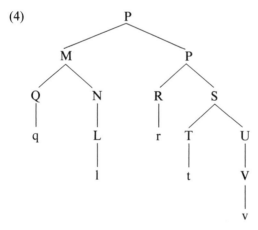

In (4) M asymmetrically c-commands R and R asymmetrically c-commands T, U, and V. Therefore, A for (4) contains $\langle M, R \rangle$, $\langle R, T \rangle$, $\langle R, U \rangle$, $\langle R, V \rangle$. From the fact that $\langle M, R \rangle$ is in A, it follows that $\langle q, r \rangle$ and $\langle l, r \rangle$ are in d(A). From the fact that $\langle R, T \rangle$ and $\langle R, U \rangle$ are in A, it follows that $\langle r, t \rangle$ and $\langle r, v \rangle$ are in d(A). In other words, all the terminals of the specifier M are on the opposite side of the head R (terminal r) from all the terminals of the complement S.

More generally put, no matter how complex the specifier or complement, it will always be the case, in any phrase marker, that specifier and complement are on opposite sides of the head. In other words, if we represent head, specifier, and complement as H, S, and C, then the conclusion so far is that of the six permutations of H, S and C, only two are permitted by the theory, namely, S-H-C and C-H-S. The other four (S-C-H, C-S-H, H-S-C, H-C-S) are all excluded by the requirement that specifier and complement be on opposite sides of the head.

The exclusion of S-C-H (e.g., of SOV) requires us to distinguish a complement position from the contents of that position. What I claim, and will return to in more detail below, is that SOV (and more generally S-C-H) is strictly impossible, in any language, if taken to indicate a phrase marker in which the sister phrase to the head (i.e., the complement position) precedes that head. On the other hand, SOV (and S-C-H) is perfectly allowable if taken to indicate a phrase marker in which the complement has raised up to some specifier position to the left of the head.

4.2   Specifier-Head-Complement as a Universal Order

We are now left with two constituent order possibilities, specifier-head-complement and complement-head-specifier. A rapid look at (a small subset of) the world's (presently existing) languages reveals that of the two orders, the former is a significantly more plausible universal than is the latter. Consideration of the relative order of head and complement alone is not sufficient to yield any firm conclusion, since both head-complement and complement-head orders are widely attested. On the other hand, the relative order of specifier and head is much more visibly asymmetric, in the following sense: although there may be some categories for which both orders are widespread, there are other categories where specifier-head order strongly predominates. (I know of no categories for which head-specifier is the cross-linguistically predominant order.)

In fact, CP is a category whose specifier, the typical landing site for moved *wh*-phrases, is visibly initial to an overwhelming degree.[1] Spec,IP (i.e., subject position) is clearly predominantly initial in its phrase.[2] That is straightforwardly true for SVO and SOV languages, and almost as obviously true for VSO languages, assuming the by now usual analysis of VSO order as deriving from SVO order by leftward V-movement.[3] According to Greenberg (1966, p. 76), the other types, OVS, OSV, and VOS, are "excessively rare."

From the present perspective, OSV would involve movement of the O past S to the specifier position of a higher head. OVS and VOS must not have S in a final specifier position, but must instead either have OV or VO moving as a unit leftward past S, or else V and O moving separately leftward past S,[4] with the expectation, then, that such languages should show OVSX and VOSX orders.

I conclude that specifier-head-complement, and not the reverse, is the only order available to the subcomponents of a phrase. Consider again, in this light, (4). The conclusion just stated that S-H-C order is the only one available means that the linear ordering d(A) containing, for example, $\langle q, r \rangle$ and $\langle l, r \rangle$ and $\langle r, t \rangle$ and $\langle r, v \rangle$ should be interpreted so that $\langle x, y \rangle$ means that the terminal symbol x *precedes* the terminal symbol y.

4.3   Time and the Universal Specifier-Head-Complement Order

This is not logically necessary. We can imagine a UG that would differ from the one I claim to be characterizing. This other UG would be identical to the actual one but would interpret $\langle x, y \rangle$ as meaning that x follows y. That would yield a perfectly valid linear ordering, one that would be the mirror image of the actual one. Languages compatible with this other UG would have C-H-S order instead of the actually valid S-H-C and would look like a set of strict mirror images of the languages we are familiar with.

I would now like to suggest a possible explanation for the fact that UG imposes S-H-C order on phrases, rather than the reverse. (The proposal will also account for the fact that UG does not allow languages a choice between S-H-C and C-H-S.) It is therefore necessary for me to explain why $\langle x, y \rangle$ is interpreted as 'x precedes y' rather than as 'x follows y'.

Recall from chapter 1 that the asymmetric c-command relation is significantly similar to the dominance relation (both are locally linear). Associated with the dominance relation on phrase markers is a "root node" that has the property of dominating every node in the phrase marker (except itself). In the usual phrase marker, no node has the property of asymmetrically c-commanding every node except itself. I would like to propose bringing asymmetric c-command and dominance more into parallel by postulating an abstract node A for every phrase marker, with the property that A asymmetrically c-commands every other node. This abstract node should be thought of as being adjoined to the root node.[5]

Since every other node dominates at least one (perhaps empty) terminal element, A should be taken to dominate a terminal element. There are two plausible candidates, either an abstract terminal a that has the property of preceding all the other terminals (i.e., an abstract beginning terminal) or an abstract terminal z that follows all the other terminals. I propose that the abstract root node for asymmetric c-command should be mapped by d into the abstract beginning terminal a.

The intuitive motivation for taking $d(A) = a$ rather than $d(A) = z$ is that a and z are not quite as symmetric as they might seem, in a way that favors a. Let us think of the string of terminals as being associated with a string of time slots. That by itself is not sufficient to induce an asymmetry between a and z. Let me then make the further claim that what is paired with each time slot is not simply the corresponding terminal, but the substring of terminals ending with that terminal (i.e., the substring produced up to that time).

In other words, a string of terminals abcdz (with a and z abstract) is mapped to a set of substrings.

(5) a, ab, abc, abcd, abcdz

An asymmetry between a and z has now appeared: a precedes every terminal in every substring, but z does not follow every terminal in every substring (since z figures in only one substring). If the abstract root node for asymmetric c-command needs to be mapped by d to a corresponding abstract "root node" for terminals, and if that root node for terminals must be in some fixed relation to every terminal in every substring, then that abstract terminal must be a and the fixed relation must be 'precedes'.

Let us consider, then, that $d(A) = a$. The question we are trying to answer is how to interpret $\langle x, y \rangle$, where $\langle x, y \rangle$ is in d(A). More specifically, the question is whether $\langle x, y \rangle$ is 'x precedes y' or 'x follows y'.

Assume the latter. Now by hypothesis the abstract node A asymmetrically c-commands Y, for all Y, so that $\langle A, Y \rangle$ is in A, for any phrase marker containing Y. Since $d(A) = a$, it follows that $\langle a, y \rangle$ is in d(A) (for all y dominated by Y). So that if $\langle x, y \rangle$ is 'x follows y', we conclude that 'a follows y', for all y. But a is the abstract beginning terminal. Thus, we have a contradiction. Therefore $\langle x, y \rangle$ cannot be 'x follows y' but must rather be 'x precedes y'.

From the fact that $\langle x, y \rangle$ is to be interpreted as 'x precedes y', it follows, as discussed in the preceding section, that the unique order of constituents

provided by UG is S-H-C, as desired. In effect, the fact that UG provides
S-H-C order (rather than the reverse) derives from the hypothesis that (5)
(rather than a sequence of substrings working backward from the final
terminal) is the correct way of representing the relation between terminals
and time slots. This S-H-C property of UG, as well as the fact that UG
does not make both orders available, is thus seen to be ultimately related
to the asymmetry of time.

4.4   Linear Order and Adjunction to Heads

We have just seen how the fact that specifiers are adjoined to the head +
complement constituent results in specifiers necessarily preceding the head
(and complement). Now consider the adjunction of one head to another,
as in (6).

(6)

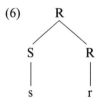

As shown in section 3.2, S asymmetrically c-commands R. Therefore,
$\langle s, r \rangle$ is in the $d(A)$ of (6). By the results of the preceding section, it
follows that s precedes r. In other words, the present theory has as a
necessary consequence that an adjoining head (S) will invariably precede
the head that it adjoins to (R).

Taking S to be a clitic, this derives the generalization that I proposed in
earlier work to the effect that a clitic invariably precedes the head that it
adjoins to.[6]

4.5   Linear Order and Structure below the Word Level

What does the present theory say about structure below the word level?
Consider a head with internal structure, as in (7).

(7) Cats overturn chairs.

The verb *overturn* consists of *over* and *turn*. The relevant VP configuration
is (8).

(8)

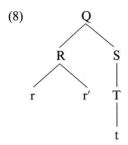

R asymmetrically c-commands T. Therefore, both r and r′ will precede t, apparently correctly. However, it is not at all clear that in a case like (7) we really want to say that there is a V node (corresponding to R) that dominates two terminals with no intervening structure whatsoever.

Let us assume, then, that rather than (8) the structure of (7) is (9).

(9)

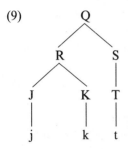

Here j and k are the two morphemes that comprise the head R, and they are dominated respectively by the sub-word-level nonterminals J and K. Now R asymmetrically c-commands T as before, so that j and k will precede t, as expected. However, S now asymmetrically c-commands J and K, so that ⟨t, j⟩ and ⟨t, k⟩ will be in d(A). Consequently, t must precede both j and k. But that is a contradiction (violation of antisymmetry). The conclusion, then, is that (9) is not a possible representation for (7).

This conclusion could be evaded if we were to decide that J and K are really different from the usual nonterminals. Put another way, we might decide that J and K here do not belong to the set of nonterminals on which is defined the relation of asymmetric c-command that in this theory maps into linear precedence. Such a decision would have the effect of divorcing sub-word-level structure from phrase structure; that is, it would have the effect of making structure below the word level invisible to the LCA.

A stronger and more interesting claim would be that there are no elements other than the usual terminals and nonterminals, that is, that J and K in (9) must come from the set of nonterminal elements on which asymmetric c-command is defined. Since (9) is not a legitimate representation for (7), another must then be available, namely, (10).

(10)

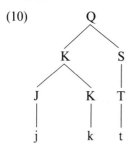

I have just replaced R by K, so that we have a head K to which another head J is adjoined. This representation turns out to be compatible with the LCA. K (and J) asymmetrically c-command T, so that j and k must precede t. The crucial point is that here S does not asymmetrically c-command either K or J (S and K, and S and J, c-command each other). Therefore, (10) yields no contradiction.

Desirous of taking the stronger position described in the preceding paragraph, I conclude that a complex verb like *overturn* in (7) must be an instance of *over* adjoining to *turn*.

The same reasoning carries over to all instances of V + affix, on the assumption that affixes are always exhaustively dominated by a nonterminal—that is, that they always belong to some syntactic category (as Williams (1981, p. 249) argues).[7] Thus, in *turns*, *turn* must be adjoined to *-s* (not surprisingly). In *overturns*, *overturn* must be adjoined to *-s* and *over* to *turn*.[8]

Williams (1981) (see also Di Sciullo and Williams 1987) has argued for the importance of the notion "head of a word." From the vantage point of (10), the following characterization suggests itself:

(11) The head of a word W is the terminal element dominated by the category W.

If a word is always an adjunction structure (whose highest segment is W— the upper K in (10)) that includes all the terminals comprising that word, then (11) picks out as unique head the terminal that is dominated by the category W. Thus, in (10) the head of the word K (=jk) is k.

Williams (1981, p. 248) argues further that the head of a word is generally its rightmost element, noting that suffixes generally determine the category of the word they are suffixes of, whereas prefixes generally do not.[9] The fact that the head of a word is rightmost in a language like English, whose syntactic heads are visibly leftmost in their minimal phrase, is, however, surprising. The present theory based on the LCA succeeds in providing an account for it, as follows.

From the discussion of (6), we know that in an adjunction structure the adjoining element must invariably precede the element adjoined to. A word is an adjunction structure, whose head, by the natural definition (11), is the element adjoined to. Therefore, the head of a word must be preceded by the rest of the word, as desired.

The idea that all subword structure is of the adjunction type appears to be too strong when certain types of compounds are taken into account, for example, the V-N type that is common in Romance.

(12) ouvre-boîte
     open can

Whereas the English counterpart *can opener* is plausibly analyzed as '[[can open] er]', with *can* adjoined to the verb *open* and the result of that adjunction adjoined in turn to the suffix *-er*,[10] the French example in (12) does not readily lend itself to a simple adjunction analysis.

It should be noted, on the other hand, that the argument given above based on (9), to the effect that a head cannot have internal structure of a nonadjoined sort, depends on the head in question having a complement (since it is the interaction between the complement and the subparts of the head that causes the problem discussed there). Now it is not implausible to claim that a verb must always have a complement (i.e., that unergative verbs have an abstract complement, as suggested in Hale and Keyser 1993, p. 54, and Kayne 1993, sec. 3.4). If so, then verbs will continue to be limited to having the adjunction type of substructure.

Compound nouns such as the one in (12) typically have no complement. Therefore, an analysis such as '$[_N [_V$ ouvre] $[_{NP} [_N$ boîte]]]' is available.[11]

Similarly, an alternative analysis of *can opener* might be '... er [open $[_{NP}[_N$ can]]]', with *open* adjoining to *-er* and the NP *can* moving to the specifier of the *-er* projection (see note 34 of chapter 3).

4.6   The Adjunction Site of Clitics

If, as suggested in the previous section, subword structure does fall under
the LCA, we must reconsider the question of where exactly clitics are
adjoined.

(13) Voi lo vedete.
      you it see
      'You see it'

In this Italian sentence the clitic precedes the finite verb, which itself ends
in a person/number agreement suffix *-te*. Both the present theory and
standard analyses take *vede-* to be adjoined to that suffix. Now by the
discussion of section 3.3 we know that multiple adjunction to a given head
is not legitimate. Consequently, the clitic *lo* in (13) cannot be adjoined to
vedete (since that would be a second adjunction to *-te*).

Although adjunction to the category headed by *-te* is not possible, there
is an obvious alternative, namely, clitic adjunction to *vede-*. This alternative would not be available, however, if *vede-* is itself composed of the
stem *ved-* adjoined to the so-called thematic vowel *-e-*. Rather, we would
have to say that the clitic is adjoined directly to the stem itself. Following
this reasoning, if the stem had a prefix adjoined to it, as in (14), then the
clitic would have to be adjoined to the prefix.

(14) Voi lo prevedete.
      you it predict
      'You predict it'

This seems unlikely, especially when combined with the fact that pronominal elements (of which clitics are one subtype) are normally excluded
from appearing within words (**it-lover*, etc.) to begin with.

I conclude that pronominal clitics should not be taken to be adjoined to
stems or prefixes, or to finite verb forms. What remains is to take these
clitics to be adjoined to empty functional heads, as I have argued to be
straightforwardly true in cases like (15) (see Kayne 1989b, part I; 1991,
sec. 1.1).

(15) en   fort   bien parler
      of-it strong well to-speak
      'to speak very well of it'

In literary French the clitic *en* can be separated from an infinitive by an
adverbial, here the equivalent of 'very well'.

To say that the same holds of (13) and (14), or their French counterparts, seems implausible at first, since separation of clitic from finite verb
by an adverb is not possible.

(16) Jean en   parle fort   bien.
      Jean of-it speaks strong well
      'Jean speaks very well of it.'

(17) *Jean en fort bien parle.

Consider the representation 'Jean en + F^0 parle', with the clitic adjoined
to a phonetically unrealized F^0 and the finite verb in the next lower functional head position, call it G^0. Assume that the subject DP *Jean* must
pass through the specifier position of G^0 on its way to Spec,F^0 (perhaps
for Case reasons). Then, by the result of section 3.4, no further adjunction to any projection of G^0 is permitted, so that (17) is excluded as
desired.

From this perspective, the contrast between (17) and (15) would be that
in the latter, infinitival example there is no subject DP that has to move up
through the specifier position of the infinitive. (Alternatively, in the infinitival case a functional head is available between F^0 and G^0 that is not
available in the finite case and through which no subject DP needs to
pass.)[12]

The idea that pronominal clitics must adjoin to abstract functional
heads rather than to (finite) verbs may provide an account of the fact
that in the Germanic strict verb-second languages the weak pronouns,
which in a number of ways are similar to Romance clitics, always seem
to count for verb-second. Were clitics truly able to adjoin to the finite
verb, one might expect that the appearance of a clitic would have no
effect on a verb-second structure, contrary to the following (German)
example:

(18) Gestern   hat sich der Hans ein Buch gekauft.
      yesterday has REFL the Hans a   book bought
      'Yesterday Hans bought himself a book.'

(19) *Gestern sich hat der Hans ein Buch gekauft.

From the present perspective, on the other hand, (19) is excluded since
sich must be adjoined to a functional head distinct from that containing
the finite verb. Consequently, the finite verb cannot be in the highest head
position, that is, in the one whose specifier *gestern* occupies, contrary to
the verb-second requirement.[13]

The incompatibility of a preverbal pronoun with verb-second seen in (19) contrasts sharply with the facts of the French construction that involves inversion of finite verb and subject clitic.

(20) Depuis quand connais-tu Anne?
     since   when know-you Anne
     'Since when do you know Anne?'

(21) Depuis quand la   connais-tu?
     since   when her know-you
     'Since when do you know her?'

The presence of preverbal *la* in (21) has no effect on the well-formedness of the inversion. If, as I have suggested, *la* is necessarily attached to a functional head position distinct from that containing the finite verb, it follows that *connais* in (21) cannot be in the highest head position there, in other words, that it is not in C^0.[14]

This conclusion has in fact been reached on other grounds by Sportiche (n.d.), who argues (against Kayne (1983a) and Rizzi and Roberts (1989)) that the French subject clitic inversion construction involves raising of V to C in LF only. He shows that by not taking the French construction to overtly mimic Germanic verb-second, a maximally straightforward account of (at least) two basic properties is achieved. The first is illustrated in (22).

(22) Depuis quand Jean la   connaît-il?
     since   when Jean her knows-he
     'Since when does Jean know her?'

In addition to the postverbal subject clitic, there can be a preverbal subject DP, unexpected if V overtly raised to C. Second, consider (23) and (24).

(23)   Est-il à Paris?
       is-he in Paris

(24) *Est Jean à Paris?

The fact that this inversion is unavailable with full subject DPs follows if V-to-C movement is the only means of deriving (24),[15] and if French lacks such movement entirely.

The idea that the subject clitic inversion construction can exist quite independently of overt V-movement to C^0 receives further support from Poletto's (1992, p. 300) observation that (certain varieties of) Piedmontese allow subject clitic inversion in the presence of an overt complementizer (in root contexts only).

Poletto (1992, p. 211) discusses a second fact that is directly relevant to my conclusion that the presence of a preverbal object clitic, as in (21), implies that the verb is not in C^0. She notes that in some Veneto dialects a preverbal negation actually blocks subject clitic inversion and proposes that in those dialects there is a Neg^0 that creates a minimality effect between the finite verb and C^0. (If Sportiche and I are correct, that effect must come into play at LF, much as in Chomsky's (1991, sec. 3.1) account of English *John not wrote.*)

On the other hand, there appears to be no Romance dialect in which a preverbal object clitic blocks subject clitic inversion. The reason is either that object clitics are never heads located in a position comparable to that of Neg^0 and/or that object clitics do not appear at LF.[16]

The preceding discussion must be extended to cover potential inversion constructions in Romance that do not involve subject clitics, for example, in Italian (with a pro subject).

(25) A chi   li   hai   dati?
     to whom them you-have given
     'To whom have you given them?'

If I am correct in taking the object clitic *li* not to be adjoined to V, its presence before the finite verb *hai* implies that the finite verb is not overtly in C^0.[17]

Imperatives offer further support for the idea that Romance clitics are never adjoined to any form of V, but only to an abstract functional head. As emphasized by Rooryck (1992), true imperative verbs in Romance precede clitics in positive imperatives, for example, in Italian.

(26) Fallo!
     do-it

Let us assume, with Rivero (1994; to appear) that in such imperatives the verb must move to C^0. Then the relative position of verb and clitic in (26) is straightforward, on the usual assumption that Romance clitics are located somewhere within IP.[18] A problem remains, though. Why couldn't the verb, in moving to C^0, carry along the clitic?

(27) *Lo fa!

As an imperative, (27) is sharply ungrammatical. A derivation of it in which the clitic would reach C^0 as a side effect of V-movement is correctly and simply excluded, given the main hypothesis of this section, namely, that pronominal clitics are never adjoined to verbs (and so cannot be carried along with them).

Rooryck (1992), whose approach to (27) in terms of relativized minimality I have not needed to adopt, suggests that the ungrammaticality of (27) is to be related to that of clitic + infinitive in Italian (and similarly for other Romance languages in which clitics follow infinitives).

(28)   Farlo   bene è importante.
       to-do it well is important

(29)   *Lo fare bene è importante.

Agreeing with his suggestion, I now take the ungrammaticality of (29) to reflect in part the fact that the Italian infinitive, in moving leftward, cannot carry along a pronominal clitic, exactly as discussed above (and in part the fact that the landing site for Italian infinitives is to the left of the position of clitics).[19]

Chapter 5

Further Consequences

5.1 There Is No Directionality Parameter

If UG unfailingly imposes S-H-C order, there cannot be any directionality parameter in the standard sense of the term. The difference between so-called head-initial languages and so-called head-final languages cannot be due to a parametric setting whereby complement positions in the latter type precede their associated heads.[1]

Instead, we must think of word order variation in terms of different combinations of movements. Note first that from the present perspective, any movement of a phrase upward to a c-commanding position must be leftward. This is so, for the simple reason that asymmetric c-command implies precedence.[2]

If syntactic theory allowed lowering a phrase to a position c-commanded by the original position, such movement would have to be rightward. If lowerings are not available at all, as Chomsky's (1993) proposals would lead one to expect, then that possibility can be set aside. (Lowerings, as well as movements to a position that neither c-commands nor is c-commanded by the original position, can be excluded by a familiar requirement to the effect that every trace of movement must be asymmetrically c-commanded by its antecedent; see Fiengo 1977.)

The picture of word order variation I arrive at, then, is the following. Languages all have S-H-C order. Languages (or subparts of languages) in which some complement precedes the associated head must necessarily have moved that complement leftward past the head into some specifier position. To take a simple example, consider prepositional phrases versus postpositional phrases. The former can be thought of as reflecting the basic order H-C. The latter cannot be. Rather, postpositional phrases must be derived by moving the complement of the adposition into the specifier position of that adposition (or of a higher functional head associated with it).

Similarly for categories other than P. In an OV language (or construction) the O must necessarily have moved leftward past the V into a higher specifier position. In a language where IP precedes C^0, IP must have moved leftward into Spec,C^0. And so on.

The preceding paragraph oversimplifies in at least one important respect. Take the category V as an example. Strictly speaking, overt OV order implies that starting from a basic VO order, the O must have moved leftward far enough to end up to the left of the position in which V ends up. The O must surface in some specifier position, but exactly how far left (i.e., how high up) that position must be will depend in part on how far left the V itself moves (by head-to-head movement). (The same is true of adpositions and their complements, though the range of possible movements is presumably substantially more limited than in the case of verbs.)

This kind of ambiguity in the term OV is of course familiar from the study of VO languages. The work of Emonds (1978), Pollock (1989), and Belletti (1990) has shown that English, French, and Italian differ in how high the V raises (and in addition there are language-internal differences between finite verbs and infinitives, at least in French). Furthermore, when V raises, O has the possibility of raising without ending up to the left of V. Thus, Pollock (1989, p. 369) argues that in (1) the object *rien* has moved farther left than an ordinary object would have.

(1) Pierre ne   mange rien.
    Pierre NEG eats   nothing

Rizzi (1991) has made a similar argument for Italian.[3]

5.2   The LCA Applies to All Syntactic Representations

The LCA imposes a tight relation between hierarchical structure and linear order. Linear order is a fundamental aspect of certain syntactic representations, in particular, those that feed into PF. However, there are other syntactic representations, notably those at LF and those at D-Structure (or the closest counterparts to D-Structure in Chomsky's (1993) framework), for which one might think that linear order is not essential. The question arises, then, whether the LCA needs to be taken to apply to all syntactic representations.

Recall that I have argued that the LCA is the source of all the major properties of phrase structure that have been attributed to X-bar theory, in other words, that X-bar theory, rather than being a primitive part of syntactic theory, actually derives from the LCA (plus the definition of c-command in terms of categories, as in (16) of chapter 3). It follows that to declare the LCA inapplicable to some level of representation—say, LF—would be to declare inapplicable to that level of representation all the restrictions on phrase structure familiar from X-bar theory (existence of at least one and at most one head per phrase, etc.). In the absence of compelling evidence to the contrary, the much more restrictive characterization of phrase structure is to be preferred. Since I see no such compelling evidence to the contrary, I conclude that the LCA does underlie the entire set of syntactic representations and therefore that every syntactic representation is automatically associated with a fixed linear ordering of its terminal symbols.

I assume further that the discussion of section 4.3 generalizes to all syntactic representations, so that the same linear order S-H-C holds for all syntactic representations, as assumed implicitly in the preceding section.

5.3   Agreement in Adpositional Phrases

Kenneth Hale (personal communication) notes that although there are languages, like Navajo, with obligatory agreement between an adposition (postposition) and its lexical complement, prepositional phrases in SVO languages never, as far as he knows, show such agreement.[4] If agreement between an adposition and its complement must reflect agreement between a head and its specifier, then we have an immediate account of this asymmetry: a postposition can agree with its lexical complement because, under an LCA-based theory, the complement of a postposition is necessarily in (or else has necessarily passed through) the relevant specifier position.

A prepositional phrase in an SVO language, on the other hand, can be taken to have a complement that has not moved at all (i.e., has not reached the relevant specifier position) and so cannot license agreement. This assumes, of course, that specifier positions are always on the left of the head. If a specifier position could be on the right, then this asymmetry would remain mysterious. Put another way, this asymmetry concerning adpositional agreement supports the result derived earlier that specifiers necessarily precede their associated head.

One might wonder whether a language could allow the following: the lexical complement of an adposition moves to the specifier position, triggering agreement,[5] after which the adposition itself raises to a higher head position,[6] yielding what looks like a prepositional phrase, with agreement. In fact, this seems to be the case in Jacaltec, to judge from observations by Craig (1977, p. 110). This leads to a conjecture, for which an explanation would be required.

(2) Agreement between a preposition and its lexical complement is
    possible only in a V ... S ... language.

Van Riemsdijk (1978) has argued that the (more productive) Dutch counterpart of English *thereof, whereby, herewith* should be analyzed as involving leftward movement of the locative to the specifier position of P. I know of no language whose Ps are normally postpositional, yet take locative complements to their right, in other words, no language that would be the mirror image of Dutch in this area of syntax. If there truly is no such language, then we have found further support for the claim that specifiers always precede their heads and complements always follow (since if complements could precede and specifiers follow, then mirror-Dutch should exist).

5.4 Head Movement

If I am correct in claiming that heads always precede their associated complement position, then head-to-head raising must invariably be leftward, since the head raised to must of necessity precede the complement whose head is to raise. Instances of leftward head movement are well known, one very clear case being that found in the verb-second constructions of the Germanic languages, in which the finite verb in (primarily) root contexts raises leftward to the highest head position, where it is preceded by the corresponding specifier.[7]

If languages were allowed the option of having complements precede heads and heads precede specifiers, then we would expect to find languages that were the mirror image of Germanic with respect to verb-second phenomena (i.e., the finite verb would move to second-from-last position in root sentences). I do not know of any such languages. If that gap is not accidental, it supports the idea that S-H-C is the only available order of constituents.

Assuming that specifiers do always precede their associated heads, it still might be the case that complements have the option of preceding their heads. If that were so, then IP could precede and be the sister of C^0. This would allow the existence of a language in which the finite verb raised to a sentence-final C^0 only in root contexts, again much as in Germanic (with Spec,CP initial). Again I know of no such language. If that is not accidental, then we again have confirmation of the idea that complement positions must invariably follow their associated heads.[8]

Greenberg's (1966, p. 94) Universal 33 states that one can find languages in which number agreement holds for '... DP_{subj} V ....', but not for '... V DP_{subj} ...'. However, according to him, there are no languages in which a following subject determines number agreement whereas a preceding subject does not. In languages of the first type, such as Arabic, number agreement is evidently sensitive to whether or not the V asymmetrically c-commands DP_{subj}; if it does, number agreement fails to hold.

The absence of languages of the second type indicates that a V cannot asymmetrically c-command a DP_{subj} that precedes it. Since V can asymmetrically c-command a subject only if it moves to a head position above that subject, this absence follows directly from the absence of rightward head movement,[9] that is, from the impossibility of having a complement position precede its head.

Banishing rightward head movement from UG reduces (a priori desirably) the number of analyses available for characterizing sentence-final 'V-T-Agr' (or similar) sequences in head-final languages. More specifically, it makes unavailable an analysis that would purport to be the mirror image of the standard analysis of 'V-T-Agr' in SVO languages like French and Italian, based on successive leftward head movement. In other words, in a head-final language a 'V-T-Agr' sequence cannot be derived by raising V rightward to T and then raising the result rightward to Agr.[10]

Two possibilities remain. The first is simply leftward head movement itself. Consider Holmberg and Platzack's (to appear) generalization to the effect that within the Scandinavian family of languages/dialects the existence of person agreement within the verbal paradigm implies the existence of V-raising to Agr_S. Assume that English is compatible with (an extrapolation of) this generalization by virtue of -s being an instance of number agreement only, as argued in Kayne 1989a. Then it would be plausible to expect their generalization to hold for Germanic in general, if not universally.[11]

Since German and Dutch show person agreement, it would follow that in those languages, too, V raises to Agr$_S$. From my perspective, this raising must be thought of as leftward, just as for Icelandic, French, and Italian. The specificity of German and Dutch lies in their requiring most of their complements to move leftward past V. Since the finite V in German and Dutch must raise to Agr$_S$,[12] by the preceding argument, I am led to conclude that in those languages the leftward-moved complements must end up to the left of the Agr$_S$ position.

That leftward movement of complements in German and Dutch does not simply take place within the V projection is reinforced by two observations. First, when the verb is infinitival, the complements must precede not only it but also the infinitival marker *zu/te*, which I take to be heading a separate projection, as with English *to*. Second, the leftward-moved complements in West Flemish precede not only the verb but also the preverbal negative clitic,[13] which is almost certainly at least as high as NegP.

If the verb has raised to Agr$_S$ in German and Dutch, and if complements have moved to the left of that position, then the subject, at least when it is to the left of one or more complements, cannot be in Spec,Agr$_S$ (in particular, in light of my argument in section 3.4 that multiple adjunction to a given category is excluded), although it presumably will have passed through it. The conclusion that subjects in German and Dutch can be, and with ordinary transitives typically are, higher than the Agr$_S$ projection may ultimately contribute to an understanding of a striking asymmetry within Germanic, namely, that complementizer agreement with the subject (see Bayer 1984; Cardinaletti and Roberts 1990; Haegeman 1990; Platzack 1992) is found only in the Germanic SOV languages, and never in the Germanic SVO languages, to the best of my knowledge. (For example, it may be that the subject DP can reach (at LF; see Law 1991) the specifier of an Agr projection higher than Agr$_S$ only in a language that overtly has subjects able to move higher than Spec,Agr$_S$.)

5.5 Final Complementizers and Agglutination

The second possibility that remains open for deriving sequences of inflectional morphemes in a "head-final" language is as follows, where X and Y are such morphemes:

(3) $\ldots$ X [$_{YP}$ $\ldots$ Y ZP] $\ldots \rightarrow \ldots$ X [$_{YP}$ ZP Y t] $\ldots \rightarrow$ [$_{YP}$ ZP Y t$_{zp}$] X t$_{yp}$ $\ldots$

Here, the sequence YX is produced by moving YP leftward to the Spec,X, subsequent to moving ZP leftward to the specifier of Y. Unlike the more familiar head-raising type of derivation discussed in section 5.4, this type of derivation based on movements of nonheads produces a YX that is not a constituent.

It may be that this is what underlies pure agglutination, that is, cases in which Y and X never fuse, even partially, contrary to what can happen in inflectional languages. Since this derivation of YX as a nonconstituent depends on both Y and X having the property of forcing their complements to move to their specifier position, and since that kind of property is dominant in the so-called head-final languages, the expectation is that agglutinative YX (where Y originates below X) will primarily be found in strongly head-final languages.[14] This seems correct, in a general way.

The only potential such case that I will pursue at all here is that of final complementizers. Assume, then, that final complementizers reflect the leftward movement of IP into Spec,CP. I will mention three apparently favorable consequences (as compared with an approach that would take IP to be base-generated as a left sister of C^0).[15]

First consider *that*-trace violations, found in a subset of complementizer-initial languages.

(4) Who did you think would win?

(5) *Who did you think that would win?

To the best of my knowledge, parallel complementizer-trace violations (where subject extraction would be possible with a covert, but not with an overt, complementizer) are not found in complementizer-final languages.

(6) (Conjecture) *That*-trace effects are found only with initial complementizers.

This would follow if a necessary condition for such violations is that the complementizer in question asymmetrically c-command the subject position, which is clearly not the case in complementizer-final languages (or constructions) if IP is in Spec,CP.[16]

Second and somewhat similar to the preceding is the question of anaphors in subject position. (The similarity is especially strong if Chomsky (1986b) is correct in holding that anaphors are subject to LF movement.) In English and other western European languages anaphors are excluded from the nominative subject position of a finite sentence. Rizzi (1990a) has suggested that the difference between these languages and Chinese, which does allow such subject anaphors, has to do with the fact that Chinese has no subject-verb agreement. This does not seem to be the right generalization, however, to judge by Yadurajan's (1988, p. 182) observation that the Dravidian languages allow subject anaphors (with the antecedent in the higher sentence). The crucial point is that some of these (e.g., Tamil and Telugu) have subject-verb agreement.[17]

An alternative generalization is that nominative anaphors in subject position are excluded from languages (or constructions) in which complementizers are initial. As in the case of *that*-trace effects, this could then be thought of in terms of asymmetric c-command: in movement terms, the raising of a nominative anaphor would be blocked by an intervening asymmetrically c-commanding C^0.[18] In effect, the movement of IP to Spec,CP would license the nominative anaphor by removing it from the c-command domain of the complementizer.

This generalization may receive further support from the fact mentioned by Harbert and Srivastav (1988, p. 80) that the Hindi reflexive cannot be the subject of a finite sentence. This is notable in that Hindi is a largely head-final language. However, finite complements have an initial complementizer *ki*, which serves as a blocking agent, if I am correct.[19]

The third potentially favorable consequence to this analysis of final complementizers lies in the area of interrogatives. Consider a language whose complementizers (or question particles) are all final. Assume as usual that interrogative *wh*-movement has Spec,CP as a landing site.[20] If a final C^0 indicates movement of IP to Spec,CP, then when a C^0 is final, it means that Spec,CP is filled and is no longer an available landing site for interrogative *wh*-movement.[21] This appears to provide a way of accounting for the fact discussed by Bach (1971, p. 161) that interrogative *wh*-movement is generally absent from SOV (i.e., from consistently head-final) languages.[22]

PART III

Chapter 6

Coordination

6.1 More on Coordination

I argued in discussing example (8) of chapter 2 that the LCA provides a principled account for the existence of coordinating conjunctions. Now consider the following well-known asymmetry:

(1) I saw John, Bill and Sam.

(2) *I saw John and Bill, Sam.

And must obligatorily appear before the last coordinated DP. The structure of (1) includes as a subpart '[Bill [and Sam]]', with *and* the head. To this, *John* can be adjoined at the left, licensed by another head, which in English can fail to be overt.

(3) [John [X^0 [Bill [and Sam]]]]

Of interest is the fact that this approach to (1) does not extend to (2), desirably.

The reason is that if we start with '[John [and Bill]]' and try to add *Sam* at the right, we come up against a violation of the result from section 4.3, to the effect that specifiers—and hence adjoined phrases, which I have argued to be indistinguishable from them—must necessarily precede the phrase that they are adjoined to. Thus, we have an account for the fact that starting with *and* as the lowest head, the grammar accommodates (1) but not (2).

The question remains why the two heads in (3) could not be interchanged, incorrectly yielding (2) in a separate way.

(4) *[John [and [Bill [X^0 Sam]]]]

The solution may lie in Munn's (1993, chap. 4) proposal (made for the case of two conjuncts) that *and* raises in LF. Adapting it to the present framework (and to the case of *n* conjuncts) leads to the following proposal: the phonetically unrealized X^0 in (3) is licensed by the LF raising of *and*. Since there is no parallel LF lowering, the phonetically unrealized X^0 of (4) fails to be licensed.

The idea that coordination takes the form '[DP_i [and DP_j]]', with the entire phrase a projection of *and*, contains two subideas that it is useful to consider separately. For example, Munn (1993) accepts the idea that '[and DP_j]' is a phrase headed by *and*, yet denies that DP_i is the specifier of that phrase. Before considering how Munn's analysis differs from the one required by the LCA, I will quickly note two points that indirectly reinforce the idea that *and* heads the phrase '[and DP_j]'. First, there are languages such as French in which *and* can appear before each conjunct.

(5) Jean connaît *et*   Paul *et*   Michel.
    Jean knows   and Paul and Michel

This supports taking *and* to be a head if the following conjecture turns out to be correct:

(6) The pattern '*and* DP *and* DP' occurs only in languages whose heads normally or largely precede their complements.

The second point is parallel to the first and depends on the fact that some languages allow *and* to appear after each conjunct, as noted for Japanese by Kuno (1973, chap. 8). For example:

(7) John *to*   Mary *to*   ga kekkonsita.
    John and Mary and *ga* married

The corresponding conjecture the truth of which would support the head status of *and* is as follows:

(8) The pattern 'DP *and* DP *and*' occurs only in languages whose heads normally or largely come to be preceded by their complements.[1]

The most straightforward hypothesis concerning the constituent structure of (5) is '[et [Paul [et Michel]]]', in which the first *et* takes as its complement the phrase headed by the second *et* (cf. (3)).[2] For (7), things are more complex. The final *to* can readily be said to have had its complement moved to its left, but that is less clearly true of the other *to*. One possibility would be to say that the initial structure is '[to_1 [John to_2 Mary]]' and that '[John to_2 Mary]' moves leftward to Spec,to_1, but that the complement *Mary* of the head to_2 actually remains unmoved.[3]

As alluded to above, Munn (1993), although arguing for a head-complement analysis of '[and DP_j]', does not take the first conjunct to be in Spec,*and*. Instead, he takes the phrase '[and DP_j]' to be right-adjoined to the first conjunct DP_i, a proposal incompatible with the present theory, which prohibits all right-adjunction. Munn's most interesting argument comes from his analysis of across-the-board (ATB) extractions as a subcase of parasitic gaps,[4] and more specifically from his claim that the necessary empty operator must land in Spec,*and*. If he is correct in claiming that ATB extractions involve an empty operator, I must reinterpret the landing site of that empty operator as being in the specifier of the (sentential) complement of *and*,[5] which would permit Spec,*and* itself to be filled by the first conjunct.

6.2   Coordination of Heads, including Clitics

There can be no coordination of heads, in the strict sense. Although '[and XP]' is a perfectly well formed constituent, '[and X^0]' is ill formed, given my assumptions. The reason is as follows. In '[and XP]', *and* (more exactly, the nonterminal immediately and exhaustively dominating *and*) asymmetrically c-commands all the subparts of XP, and therefore *and* precedes all the corresponding terminals dominated by XP. No problem arises. In '[and X^0]', on the other hand, *and* (i.e., the nonterminal, as above) and X^0 c-command each other, so that neither asymmetrically c-commands the other, with the result that *and* and the terminal dominated by X^0 end up in no precedence relation whatsoever, in violation of the LCA, exactly as in the discussion of (2) of chapter 2.

The conclusion that heads cannot be coordinated is not usual. It does, however, immediately account for the fact that Romance clitics cannot in general be coordinated, as, for example, in French.

(9) a. *Jean te   et   me voit souvent.
       Jean you and me sees often
    b. *Je le   et   la   vois souvent.
       I him and her see often

On the assumption that clitics are heads, the ungrammaticality of (9) now follows directly.

Benincà and Cinque (1990) note, on the other hand, that some French speakers accept some examples parallel to (9) (my "?").

(10) ?Je lui   et   vous   ferais   un plaisir.
     I him_{DAT} and you_{DAT} would-do a pleasure

But these speakers do not accept coordination of postverbal clitics.

(11) *Donne-moi et   lui   un livre.
      give   me and him a book

I interpret the contrast between (10) and (11) to mean that constituents of the form '[Cl and Cl]' are in fact impossible, as predicted by the LCA plus the X^0 status of clitics, and that (10) is actually to be grouped with so-called right-node-raising (RNR) sentences such as (12).

(12) Mary saw and John heard the play I mentioned to you.

    I will return briefly to RNR in section 6.4 below. For present purposes, it will suffice to take RNR to involve an empty category linked to the "raised" constituent.

(13) Mary saw $[e]_i$ and ... [the play ...$]_i$

From this perspective, (10) has the representation shown in (14).[6]

(14) je lui $[e]_i$ et ... [ferais un plaisir$]_i$

The point is, now, that an RNR approach does not generalize at all to (11), assuming that the empty category in question must necessarily, in the RNR construction, precede its licenser. Whereas (10) is like (12) in that an empty category preceding the conjunction suffices to reestablish a first conjunct of normal appearance, the same does not hold of (11), in which an empty (verbal) category would have to follow the con-junction. Put another way, (10) is to (12) as (11) is to (15), which is ungrammatical:

(15) *Mary saw [the play$]_i$ and John heard $[e]_i$.

    The exclusion via the LCA of '[Cl [and Cl]]' carries over directly to '[DP_{lex} [and Cl]]', since the subconstituent *and Cl* will yield the same viola-tion as before (neither *and* nor the clitic will properly precede the other, given the lack of asymmetric c-command).[7]

(16) *Ma soeur voit souvent Jean et   les.
      my sister sees often   Jean and them

(17) *Ma soeur Jean et les voit souvent.

These are both excluded, then, with *Jean et les* taken as a constituent. (17)

also needs to be excluded as an instance of RNR, with the following representation:

(18) ma soeur Jean [e]$_i$ et ... [voit souvent]$_i$

This is in fact correctly excluded, since it has the object *Jean* preposed to the (empty) finite VP/IP, in the manner of a clitic, which is not permitted.

(19) *Ma soeur Jean voit souvent.

The preceding discussion depended on the head status of clitics in their derived position. If, as suggested in section 5.2, the LCA applies to all representations, then it must be the case that a clitic does not originate as a pure head that is the complement of the verb, but rather as a subpart of the complement, as in Esther Torrego's proposal (see the discussion in Uriagereka, n.d.) that clitics originate as determiners of some sister NP: '[V [D NP]]', where NP is pro. This source for clitics, which straightforwardly avoids the problem of having two X^0 sisters, is particularly plausible if Uriagereka (1988) is correct in his claim that Galician displays movement of D^0 out of DP even when NP is lexical.[8]

My general claim that heads can never be coordinated leads me to say that the following sentence can only be an instance of RNR:

(20) John criticized and insulted his boss.

That is, the structure must include an empty category.

(21) John criticized [e]$_i$ ... [his boss]$_i$

This is supported, I think, by the feeling that (20) is slightly less than perfectly natural, as compared with the corresponding sentence with a longer object.

(22) John criticized and insulted the very person who had helped him.

Furthermore, (20) seems appreciably the same as (23), which clearly does not have 'V *and* V'.[9]

(23) John criticized and then insulted his boss.

Another kind of example that might lead one to think in terms of X^0-coordination is (24).[10]

(24) my friend and colleague John Smith

Here, there is reference to only one individual. But the same is true of (25).

(25) my friend from high school and beloved colleague John Smith

Since *friend from high school* is not a lexical category, it is virtually certain that this construction involves NP-, not N^0-, coordination (with a common D^0), even in (24).[11]

In Kayne 1975, sec. 2.5, n. 37, I suggested that French might provide evidence for some notion of compound verb. The relevant data involve coordinate structures in which there are two verbs and one clitic that corresponds to a complement of each verb.

(26) Jean vous   parlera   et   vous   pardonnera.
      Jean you$_{DAT}$ will-speak and you$_{DAT}$ will-forgive
      'Jean will speak to you and forgive you.'

(27) *Jean vous parlera et pardonnera.

Put another way, the ungrammatical sentence (27) has one clitic for two gaps. From Munn's (1993) perspective, this ungrammaticality should be (partially) relatable to the fact that French clitics do not normally license parasitic gaps.[12] I noted then that although (27) is the typical case, there are exceptions such as (28).

(28) Paul les   lit   et   relit   sans   cesse.
      Paul them reads and rereads without stop
      'Paul reads and rereads them incessantly.'

The grammaticality of (28) seems to depend on the fact that the two verbs are closely related. The question is whether or not (28) is best thought of as an instance of V-coordination limited to cases of closely related Vs.

Even this minimal amount of X^0-coordination would be excluded by the LCA, correctly, I think. Relevant evidence comes from Benincà and Cinque's (1990) observation that (28) is possible only with a preverbal clitic. If the clitic is postverbal, as it is in French in positive imperatives, then the corresponding sentence with one clitic for two complements is impossible.

(29) *Lis- et   relis-les!
      read and reread them

This contrast between (28) and (29) recalls the contrast discussed above between (10) and (11) and suggests an approach along the following lines. French and Italian clitics are not normally viable identifiers for the empty operator that would be needed (in the second conjunct and binding the second object position, from Munn's (1993) perspective) to make (27) acceptable. When the two verbs are sufficiently similar,[13] but not otherwise, the empty operator can be reinterpreted as an empty clitic having the overt clitic as its antecedent (traces in object position not indicated).

(30) Paul les$_i$ lit et [e]$_i$ relit sans cesse

Assuming that the antecedent of the empty clitic must precede it and/or c-command it (possible if the overt clitic of (30) has moved out of the coordinate structure entirely), it follows, as desired, that there can be no comparably legitimate representation for (29).

The severe limitations on the possibility of having one clitic for two verbs thus support the claim made by the LCA that heads cannot be coordinated. If V-coordination were straightforwardly available, as is commonly assumed, then French and Italian sentences like (27) should be productively acceptable, contrary to fact.

6.3 Coordination with *With*

Lakoff and Peters (1969) argue that the grammar should express the relation between pairs of sentences like (31) and (32) transformationally.

(31) John and Bill collided.

(32) John collided with Bill.

That the latter contains a coordinate subject at some level of representation is supported by the plural *friends* in (33), which would thereby be licensed in a natural way.

(33)   John is friends with Bill.

(34) *John is friends.
        (vs. the possible *John is a friend*)

Lakoff and Peters (p. 127) propose that (32) should be derived from (31) by the application of a rule replacing *and* by *with*, followed by movement of the newly created *with*-phrase to a position right-adjoined to VP.

If Lakoff and Peters's proposal for a transformational relation in the above case is wrong, and if the *with*-phrase should instead be considered some kind of verbal complement, then (32) and (33) are not of any special interest to the LCA.

Yet Lakoff and Peters's proposal seems plausible, especially in light of Kuno's (1973, p. 117) observation that Japanese *to* corresponds both to English *and* and to English *with*, and his suggestion that this fact is not likely to be accidental (cf. Payne 1985, p. 29). I would therefore like to briefly consider how Lakoff and Peters's analysis might be rethought.

The first point, of course, is that right-adjunction (to any category) is prohibited by the present LCA-based theory, so that Lakoff and Peters's right-adjunction of the *with*-phrase to VP cannot be adopted. Thinking rather of Sportiche's (1988) reanalysis of rightward quantifier floating as leftward quantifier stranding, and of the now widely accepted idea that subjects originate within VP, I would like to reinterpret (32)/(33) as involving stranding of the *with*-phrase as the result of leftward movement of *John* out of a constituent *John with Bill*.

In English it seems clear that the first conjunct *John* of a phrase like *John and Bill* is adequately Case-licensed if the phrase as a whole is Case-licensed. Let me now propose that *John with Bill* can also be generated as a coordinate phrase, with the crucial difference that the first conjunct cannot be adequately Case-licensed simply by virtue of the whole phrase being in a licensing position. In other words, if the coordinating element is *with*, the first conjunct must move out of the coordinate phrase and reach a Case-licensing position by itself. (The second conjunct will be Case-licensed by *with*.)

Thus, in (32) the thematic subject position within VP will initially be filled by the phrase *John with Bill*. The first conjunct *John* will move out of that phrase and end up in Spec,IP, where it will receive Case. From this perspective, the contrast between a conjoined phrase headed by *and* and a conjoined phrase headed by *with* is analogous to the contrast with respect to Case in English between a gerund with an initial lexical subject and a *to* + infinitive phrase with an initial lexical subject. Put another way, (35)–(37) are ungrammatical for the same reason (lack of Case on *John*).[14]

(35) *John with Bill will collide.

(36) *John to go away would be a good idea.

(37) *John intelligent is believed by everyone.

The same holds for (38)–(40).

(38) *I consider John with Bill to have collided.

(39) *I consider John to go away to be a good idea.

(40) *I consider John intelligent to be widely believed.

Raising of *John* to subject position in passives is precluded in all of these cases.

(41) *John is considered with Bill to have collided.

(42) *John is considered to go away to be a good idea.

(43) *John is considered intelligent to be widely believed.

The greater strength of the violation here may be due to an Empty Category Principle (ECP) effect triggered by the barrierhood of the phrase in embedded subject position (*with*-phrase/infinitive phrase with *to*/adjectival small clause).

The parallelism between these coordinate *with*-phrases on the one hand and infinitivals and small clauses on the other extends further still. Small clauses in particular generally cannot be complements of prepositions. An example of this involving resultatives is discussed in Kayne 1985, p. 123.[15]

(44)   The boy squashed the insect flat.

(45) *The boy stepped on the insect flat.

Now consider sentences with *between*, which might well be thought to lend themselves to the *and*/*with* alternation, in that they are instances of phrasal and not sentence coordination, in Lakoff and Peters's (1969) sense. Yet they do not permit *with*.

(46)   John stood between Bill and Paul.

(47) *John stood between Bill with Paul.

If *Bill with Paul* is a subvariety of small clause, then the ungrammaticality of (47) falls together with that of (45), just as the grammaticality of (48) falls together with that of (44).

(48) John compared Bill with Paul.

Lakoff and Peters (p. 120) note that the *and*/*with* alternation is limited to cases of phrasal coordination, as opposed to sentential coordination. For example, (33) has no counterpart (49).

(49) *John is human beings with Bill.

Their transformational rule that replaces *and* by *with* provides no natural account of this fact, that is, of the correlation between the ungrammaticality of (49) and the interpretive status of (50), whose only interpretation is that of *John is a human being and Bill is a human being* (contrasting with the phrasal/group interpretation of *John and Bill are friends*).

(50) John and Bill are human beings.

From the present perspective, an interesting possibility emerges, related to the following contrast:

(51) *Both John and Bill collided.

(52) Both John and Bill knew French.

When preceding an *and*-phrase, *both* necessarily imposes the distributive reading associated with sentential coordination. The same holds of objects.

(53) *I compared both John and Bill.

(54) I saw both John and Bill.

Assume that to receive a distributive/sentential reading, a coordinate phrase (whether headed by *and* or by *with*) must be preceded by a distributor, which can be abstract (i.e., phonetically unrealized).[16] Consequently, in a sentence like (49) or (50), whose predicate allows only the distributive interpretation, a distributor is necessarily present. In the latter case this obviously causes no problem, since an overt distributor is possible (*Both John and Bill are human beings*). In the former however, it does, as follows.

   (33) has the representation shown in (55).

(55) John$_i$ is friends [[e]$_i$ with Bill]

By the argument of the preceding paragraph, (49) could not have the same representation, since (49) requires a covert distributor (to be noted BOTH).

(56) John is human beings [BOTH [[e]$_i$ with Bill]]

This representation will yield a violation, however, as desired, if BOTH induces a barrier to the movement of *John*. In other words, the incompatibility of *with* with the distributive/sentential interpretation of coordination can be taken to follow from the fact that (1) the first conjunct of the *with*-phrase must move out, for Case reasons, and (2) the distributive interpretation depends on the presence of an element BOTH that blocks that extraction.[17]

   In conclusion to this section, then, the *with* of (55) and similar sentences might be introducing a verbal or adjectival complement, in which case there would be little here of direct relevance to the present theory. If, on the other hand, this *with* is to be related to *and*, the analysis given above provides a way to express that relation without any recourse to right-adjunction.[18]

6.4 Right Node Raising

The construction in (57) has often been analyzed in terms of a rule called right node raising (RNR) that right-adjoins a copy of the "shared" constituent to the coordinate constituent, as, for example, in Postal 1974, p. 126.

(57) Mary sold and John bought a large number of books.

Since the present theory forbids right-adjunction, I must, in agreement with Wexler and Culicover (1980, pp. 298–303), McCawley (1982), Levine (1985), and McCloskey (1986), reject this analysis.

   McCawley's proposal to allow discontinuous constituent structure is in general not compatible with the present theory. In the case of (57) it amounts to the claim that *a large number of books* is dominated by the sentential node that minimally dominates *Mary sold*. Since that sentential node asymmetrically c-commands the constituents following it, including, for example, the verb *bought*, then *a large number of books* should precede *bought*, which it does not. (Recall that mutual c-command between coordinated constituents would lead to a violation of antisymmetry.)

   Wexler and Culicover propose a deletion analysis of (57) whereby the object in the first conjunct is deleted under identity with the object in the second conjunct. This analysis is compatible with the LCA and I will adopt it here, although it (like McCawley's proposal) leaves open the question of why the reverse is not permitted.

(58) *Mary sold a large number of books and John bought.

(More precisely, Wexler and Culicover's analysis excludes (58) by having the structural description of the deletion rule specify that the phrase to be deleted must be adjacent to *and*.)

   The deletion analysis of (57) differs sharply from the right-adjunction analysis in taking *a large number of books* to occupy a complement position of *bought*.[19] It therefore provides an immediate account of the fact that Dutch does not permit the equivalent of (57) with the object following an embedded V position (example from Teun Hoekstra).

(59) *Jan heeft gekocht en   Marie heeft verkocht de spullen
      Jan has   bought and Marie has   sold   the things
      waarmee zij   rijk werden.
      wherewith they rich became

If *de spullen* ... could be right-adjoined to the coordinate constituent, the deviance of (59) would not automatically follow from the fact that Dutch DP complements can in general not follow an embedded V.

(60) *Jan heeft gekocht de spullen.

Under the deletion analysis, on the other hand, (59) and (60) both reflect the need for Dutch DPs to move leftward past the embedded V.

Chapter 7

Complementation

7.1 Multiple Complements and Adjuncts

The LCA does not permit a head to have more than one complement (since the two complements would asymmetrically c-command subparts of each other and produce a violation of antisymmetry). Consider in this light the following sentence:

(1) John gave a book to the child.

A book and *to the child* cannot both be complements (i.e., sisters) of the verb. Furthermore, the structure '[[gave a book] to the child]' is excluded because right adjunction is not available.

The present theory thus derives the small clause analysis of (1) (i.e., '[gave [a book to the child]])', plus the fact that the small clause must have a head (if it did not, the antisymmetry requirement would again be violated).[1]

Consider further (2).

(2) John bought a book on Sunday.

By exactly the same reasoning as in the case of (1), we derive the conclusion that in (2) '[a book on Sunday]' must be a headed constituent. Put another way, we derive from first principles Larson's (1988; 1990) analysis of postcomplement adjuncts as phrases that are themselves in a complement position with respect to some head. (The category label of that head is a separate question; see note 1.)

This analysis of postcomplement adjuncts leads to a question concerning control. Consider (3).

(3) John criticized Bill after giving a talk on syntax.

The controller of the understood subject of *giving* is the matrix subject *John* and cannot be the matrix object *Bill*. Williams (1975) has made a proposal in terms of c-command. Starting from the standardly assumed constituent structure in which the *after*-clause is higher in the tree than the direct object, the proposal is that this kind of control requires that the controller c-command the embedded PRO. From my perspective, the *after*-clause is asymmetrically c-commanded by both the direct object and the subject, so that the reason for the interpretive asymmetry in (3) must be of a different sort.[2]

It might be, for example, that the PRO of (3) is a subject-oriented anaphor that needs to move at LF to the matrix Agr_S, in the spirit of Chomsky (1986b, p. 175) (see Hestvik 1992 and references cited there). The idea of taking certain instances of PRO to be subject-oriented anaphors is also appealing in the following case of complementation in French:

(4) Jean a dit à Paul être très fatigué.
    Jean has said to Paul to-be very tired
    'Jean has told Paul that he is very tired.'

French has many examples of infinitives approximately paraphrasable by indicatives, as in (4). (English has many fewer, one example being *John claims to be tired*.) Some of the matrix verbs compatible with this construction take an additional complement, almost always an indirect object,[3] as here. Gross (1975, pp. 76–77) observes that with these indicative-like infinitives the controller is invariably the subject, never the complement. The contrast is sharp between these and infinitives paraphrasable with subjunctives, where an indirect object controller is perfectly possible.

(5) Jean a dit à Paul de partir.
    Jean has said to Paul *de* to-leave
    'Jean has told Paul to leave.'

This control difference can be expressed by saying that in French the PRO subject of indicative-like infinitives is a subject-oriented anaphor (as opposed to the PRO of subjunctive-like infinitives).[4]

Somewhat similar to this control question is that of parasitic gaps. Consider (6) and (7).

(6) ?Who did you hire after you talked to?

(7) *Who went home after you talked to?

If this distinction is to be attributed to 0-subjacency, as suggested by Chomsky (1986a, p. 65), then it appears to be neutral between the standard view that *after*-clauses are attached higher than objects and the LCA-imposed analysis whereby (as in Larson's work) *after*-clauses are complements asymmetrically c-commanded by objects.

On the other hand, the distinction between (6) and (7) cannot be one of simple c-command (see Chomsky 1986a, pp. 60ff.), given Larson's analysis of adjuncts, unless the adjunct in (6) has raised leftward past the position of the object variable, in the manner of section 7.2. (One might also, in part in the spirit of the c-command approach, take the empty operator associated with parasitic gaps to be a pronominal with the property of Norwegian possessive pronouns, which can take an object antecedent, but not a subject antecedent. The requisite generalization of Hestvik's (1992, p. 573) analysis would be that the parasitic operator must move to the matrix Agr_S in both (6) and (7); being subject to Condition B, it triggers a violation in the latter.)

Depictive adjuncts of the following sort are standardly taken to be attached higher than the object:

(8) John left the party angry.

The present theory implies, rather, that they are attached lower than the object. Although I will leave the study of this kind of adjunct largely in abeyance, I will note two pieces of evidence supporting the latter view. First, it seems to me that a negated object can license an instance of *any* within the adjunct.

(9) John left none of the parties any more unsure of himself than he usually is.

Second, quantifier binding from the object to the adjunct seems possible.

(10) John left every party angry at the person who had organized it.

7.2 Heavy NP Shift

The prohibition against rightward adjunction that I have argued for makes no distinction between base-generated adjunctions and derived adjunctions. Consequently, no movement rule can adjoin anything to the right of anything.

This prohibition excludes a number of familiar transformations, notably here heavy NP shift, which has already been argued not to exist by

Larson (1988; 1990), who proposes an alternative analysis in terms of what he calls light predicate raising. Consider a case like (11).

(11) John gave to Bill all his old linguistics books.

Larson's analysis starts from a structure of the form '...[$_V$ e] [all his old linguistics books [gave to Bill]]' and moves the constituent '[gave to Bill]' (a V′ reanalyzed as a V) into the higher empty V position. This produces a derived structure in which '[gave to Bill]' is sister to '[all his old linguistics books ...]'. By having two complex constituents as sisters in a configuration that is not one of adjunction, the resulting structure violates the antisymmetry requirement imposed by the LCA. In other words, Larson's light predicate raising is not compatible with the present theory.

Let me therefore propose another reinterpretation of heavy NP shift, one that agrees with Larson's in taking this construction to involve leftward, not rightward, movement, but differs from his with respect to the question of what exactly is moved leftward. The basic idea is to think of English sentences like (11) as instances of scrambling of the sort found robustly in German,[5] the difference being that in English the verb ends up to the left of both complements, whereas in the corresponding German sentences the verb ends up to their right. More specifically, the proposal is that *to Bill* in (11) is moved leftward independently of V-movement. The PP *to Bill* originates in a small clause whose specifier position is filled by *all his old linguistics books* (essentially as in Larson's proposal). However, that PP moves by itself (without the verb) leftward past the object to a still higher specifier position.[6]

(12) John gave [[to Bill]$_i$ [X^0 [[all ... books] [Y^0 [e]$_i$ ...

A major advantage of a leftward movement reinterpretation of heavy NP shift is that it provides an immediate account of the following well-known restriction (often discussed in terms of Ross's (1967) Right Roof Constraint):

(13)   The fact that John gave to Bill all his old linguistics books is irrelevant.

(14)   *The fact that John gave to Bill is irrelevant all his old linguistics books.

In the absence of rightward adjunction, the only way to derive (14) would be to generate *all ... books* as complement of the matrix predicate. But that produces a straightforward theta-violation (both in the matrix, since *irrelevant* has no appropriate theta-role to assign to *all ... books*, and in the embedded sentence, since one of the theta-roles associated with *give* cannot be assigned properly). Furthermore, the fact that (14) violates theta-requirements (rather than constraints on movement) appears to provide an account of its particularly strong degree of deviance, if not near incomprehensibility.

A second advantage of the present approach is seen in Dutch and German, which by and large lack heavy NP shift to postverbal position (see Groos and Van Riemsdijk 1981, p. 184; Hirschbühler and Rivero 1983, p. 515). In the absence of right-adjunction, this can be interpreted as related to the general fact that direct objects in Dutch and German must raise leftward to a position higher than the surface position of the verb (setting aside verb-second constructions). A theory that countenanced right-adjunction would, on the other hand, have difficulty explaining why right-adjunction of the direct object to VP or IP was unavailable to precisely those languages.

A third general advantage of a scrambling approach to heavy NP shift lies in the fact that objects of prepositions cannot be "heavy-NP-shifted."

(15) *John was talking to about linguistics one of my very oldest
       friends.

From the present perspective, the correct way to think of (15) is as reflecting the fact that—not surprisingly—leftward scrambling cannot place the scrambled constituent inside a prepositional phrase between the preposition and the complement.

The status of (15) is relevant to that of (16) (from Chomsky 1982, p. 67.)

(16) John offended by not recognizing immediately his favorite uncle
       from Cleveland.

Such examples are usually taken to be instances of parasitic gaps licensed by heavy NP shift, in a way sharply incompatible with the present theory, since my reinterpretation of heavy NP shift as leftward scrambling denies that the object *his favorite uncle from Cleveland* has moved in this example and thereby denies the possibility of having a parasitic gap just after *offended*. (If there were a gap in that position, it would asymmetrically c-command the lexical object, the opposite of the usual parasitic gap configuration.) That the usual analysis of (16) is not correct, and that (16) is in fact not even an instance of the heavy NP shift construction, is suggested by examples like (17).

(17) John listened to without recognizing immediately his favorite Beethoven sonata.

This seems to have the same status as (16), but it cannot be a case of heavy NP shift because of the preposition *to*, which would be incompatible with that construction, as seen in (15). Instead, in agreement with Postal (1993, n. 12) and Williams (1990), I take (17), and hence (16), to be an instance of right node raising.

It is often said that nothing can be extracted from the direct object of a structure like (12)[7] and that this is somehow related to rightward movement. Although many examples of such extraction are indeed deviant, I do not think that the generalization is accurate, given the following construction, which I find acceptable:

(18) the problem which I explained to John only part of

To the extent that extraction in (18) is more difficult than in canonical cases like (19), the present proposal could attribute the difference to the effect of the intervening PP present between V and the direct object in (18), but not in (19).

(19) the problem which I understand only part of

To my ear, the extraction violation in (20) is stronger and more consistently found than the one in (18).

(20) *the person who(m) John gave to all his old linguistics books

From the present perspective, the violation in (20) is parallel to that found in Dutch, where P-stranding from a PP scrambled leftward from its normal position is generally not possible.[8]

The question arises whether the direct object in (12) and (18) is in the same position, hierarchically speaking, as direct objects normally are in English. Although I will not pursue this question, it is tempting to think that the answer is no—that the direct object is in fact lower than the normal direct object position. Put another way, it may be that the direct object in (12) and (18) has failed to raise as far as it otherwise would have in the absence of a preceding scrambled phrase (PP).[9] This line of thought would be particularly interesting if one could claim that the position to which direct objects normally raise in English is a Case-licensing position[10] and that it is the lack of raising, through the consequent lack of overt Case licensing, that is responsible for the heaviness/focus requirement on the direct object in (18) and similar sentences.

The familiar heaviness/focus requirement is found in English not only when verb and direct object are separated by a PP but also when there is an intervening adverb.

(21) John reread carefully all his old linguistics books.

By parity of reasoning, this should have the analysis indicated in (22).

(22) ... reread [[carefully]$_i$ [X^0 [[all ... books] [Y^0 [[e]$_i$ ...

The initial small clause structure, with the adverb as complement of the head (Y^0) that the direct object is specifier of, is as in Larson's work. The leftward movement of the adverb parallels that of the PP in (12)/(18) and simultaneously recalls leftward adverb scrambling in German. In addition, we know that adverbs can be moved leftward in *wh*-constructions, so that the leftward movement indicated in (22) is perfectly plausible.[11]

(23) How carefully did John read your article?

The preposing of the PP in (18) is reminiscent of a French construction mentioned in Kayne 1975, chap. 1, n. 81.

(24)
?J'aurais,   à ces   garçons-là, permis   de fumer   une cigarette.
I would-have to those boys there permitted *de* to-smoke a   cigarette

Here the landing site of the leftward-moved PP is to the left of and above the participle. This French construction has the property that such preposing is prohibited with direct objects.

(25) *J'aurais,   Jean, invité à la soirée.
     I would-have Jean invited to the party

This contrast between (24) and (25) recalls Cinque's (1990, p. 71) discussion of Italian clitic left-dislocation (possible without a clitic with PPs but not with direct objects) and might be explicable in the way he proposes, if subjects originate in a position below the preparticipial landing site.

Of interest to the question of heavy NP shift and its reinterpretation in terms of leftward movement is the similarity between (24)/(25) and the following English construction:

(26) Mary spoke to John, but she didn't to Bill.

(27) ?Mary criticized John, but she didn't Bill.

Whatever the absolute judgments on these, it is clear that the first is easier to accept.[12] The similarity to the French construction can be expressed if we take this VP-subdeletion in English to involve what could be called inner topicalization.

(28) ... she didn't [[to Bill] X^0 [$_{VP}$ ...

The PP is moved leftward to a position above VP[13] (whose internal structure in this construction is left open). The lesser acceptability of the corresponding direct object example is to be thought of as related to the (sharper) deviance of (25). This analysis of (26), which establishes a partial similarity between (26) and (11), allows an account of a fact noted by Kuno (1975, p. 162), namely, that (26)–(27) cannot be used as felicitous answers to questions, as follows:

(29) Who did Mary speak to? She spoke/*did to John.

From the perspective of (28), this fact is comparable to (30).

(30) Who did Mary speak to? *To John she spoke.

Although *To John she spoke* is grammatical, it is not possible in the context given in (30). The generalization that seems to hold in standard English is that (apart from interrogatives and clefts) leftward-moved phrases cannot be interpreted as focused. In Chomsky's (1976) terms, they are not subject to successful LF movement. Correspondingly, heavy NP shift, VP-subdeletion, and topicalization share the property seen (for the first of these) in (20).

(31)   I'm not sure who Mary spoke to, but I (do) know who Bill
        spoke/*did to.

(32)   *Who did you say that to, Mary had already spoken?

In each of these three constructions the preposition of the leftward-moved PP cannot be stranded.

The heaviness/focus requirement on the direct object that holds for (11) and (21) is not found in (33), even though the verb is separated there, too, from the direct object.

(33) John picked up the book.

If the suggestion is correct that the direct object in sentences like (18) and (21) is lower than the normal direct object position, then *the book* in (33) must be in a position higher than that of the direct object in (11), (18), or (21). In any event, the analysis of (33) given in Kayne 1985 must be partially incorrect, since it depended on right-adjunction (of *the book* to V').

On the other hand, the basic idea of that article, namely, that particle constructions are instances of small clauses, is straightforwardly compatible with the present theory. Thus, (34) can be analyzed as containing a small clause headed by the particle, with *the book* in the specifier position of that small clause.

(34) John picked the book up.

As far as (33) is concerned, Koopman's (1993b) analysis of Dutch particles as incorporating into V could be transposed to English, if we assume with her that following incorporation, the V can excorporate from the 'P + V' constituent. Then, starting from a structure approximately like (34), incorporation would yield an intermediate (*)*John uppicked the book*. Excorporation (see Roberts 1991) of V to a higher head position would give (33).[14]

Just as (33) must not involve right-adjunction, so Romance subject inversion must not involve right-adjunction of the subject to VP (or to any other category). Thus, an analysis of (35) in which the subject DP is right-adjoined to VP (see Rizzi 1990b, p. 63) is not possible.

(35) Ha telefonato Gianni.
     has telephoned Gianni

Rather, as noted by Belletti (1990, p. 112), even when the verb is participial, the order verb-subject can be compatible with a structure in which the subject is left-adjoined to VP (in present terms, is in the specifier of some functional head above VP), as long as the (participial) verb moves high enough. Since Belletti (1990) shows convincingly that Italian verbs, including participles, move substantially higher than their initial position, I take *Gianni* in (35) to be in a left-hand specifier position lower than (asymmetrically c-commanded by) the participle *telefonato*.[15]

Subject inversion is more limited in French than in Italian, but the same question arises for those cases in which French does admit it. For example:

(36) Quand a   téléphoné Jean?
     when has telephoned Jean

Although French past participles raise less robustly than Italian ones, I will take the participle in (36) to have moved high enough to asymmetrically c-command the (left-hand) specifier position in which the subject *Jean* is found.[16]

7.3 Right-Dislocations

The prohibition against right-adjunction that I have argued must hold does not seem to allow for right-dislocations.

(37) He's real smart, John.

I would like to suggest a link with the following construction:

(38) He's real smart, John is.

(38) clearly involves two clauses, the second of which is reduced. The fact that *he* and *John* are coreferential distinguishes this construction sharply from the following, where comparable coreference is not possible:

(39) *He$_i$ thinks John$_i$ is (smart).

(40) *?He$_i$ left when John$_i$ could.

I propose, then, that in (38) *John is* is a (reduced) clause that has *he's real smart* left-adjoined to it (with an empty functional head mediating that adjunction).[17]

(41) [[he's real smart] [X^0 [John is ...]]]

The reduction in (38) is of the familiar VP-deletion type.[18] It may be now that (37) is essentially parallel to (38) except for a more extensive reduction.[19]

(42) [[he's real smart] [X^0 [John ...]]]

The asymmetry between left-adjunctions (licit) and right-adjunctions (illicit) that the LCA-based theory imposes has thus led to a significant asymmetry between left-dislocations and right-dislocations, in the sense that the former, unlike the latter, do not require as novel an analysis. In other words, a left-dislocation such as (43) can have the analysis shown in (44).

(43) John, he's real smart.

(44) [John [X^0 [he's real smart]]]

Except for the necessary presence of an abstract X^0, this is not terribly different from, for example, Cinque's (1990) treatment of what he calls clitic left-dislocation.

The treatment of (37) in terms of the construction illustrated in (38) is not the only one that can be imagined. For the Romance languages, especially, a rather different approach to right-dislocation comes to mind, which I will now explore briefly.

The following is a typical (French) example:

(45) Jean la   voit souvent, Marie.
     Jean her sees often   Marie

The direct object *Marie* occurs in the presence of a corresponding clitic *la*. There is an intonation contour specific to dislocation constructions (and similar to that of (37)) that is indicated by the comma placed before the dislocated phrase *Marie*.

It is usually assumed that the intonation contour in question and the presence of the extra clitic go together. However, Antinucci and Cinque (1977) and more explicitly Benincà (1988a, p. 146) show that in Italian right-dislocation the clitic is actually optional.

(46) Lo porto domani,   il   dolce.
     it I-bring tomorrow the sweet

(47) Porto domani, il dolce.

Both of these are possible, pronounced with the same characteristic right-dislocation intonation.[20]

Once we see that right-dislocation does not depend on the presence of a clitic doubling an object, we are led to ask the converse question: does the doubling clitic in (46) depend on the right-dislocation intonation? The standard answer is yes, based on the fact that without this characteristic intonation (46) is not possible.

(48) *Lo porto domani il dolce.

However, Cinque (1990, p. 178) notes that in some cases (more exactly, in the presence of another object clitic) a dative clitic can double a lexical DP with normal intonation, in colloquial Italian.

(49) Glielo   dico a suo fratello.
     him$_{DAT}$ + it I-say to his brother

The right-dislocation counterpart is also possible.

(50) Glielo dico, a suo fratello.

I would like to propose that the standard answer is wrong not only for (50) but in general, and that the doubling found with right-dislocation and the doubling found in (49) constitute a single phenomenon.

Put another way, clitic doubling of the sort familiar from Spanish, and which we see in colloquial Italian in (49), is substantially less different from right-dislocation than is usually assumed. The correct way to think of the two constructions is that they in fact share clitic doubling, and instead differ from each other in a separate way, namely, with respect to the intonational/interpretive status of the lexical DP. From this perspective, (50) is to (49) as (47) is to (51).

(51) Porto il dolce.

The proposed view of right-dislocation results in a more unified picture of the Romance languages. They now all allow clitic doubling, even French, as seen in (45). Given the broad similarity among object clitics of the various Romance languages, it was never clear why clitic doubling should have been limited to only some of them. Furthermore, the idea that French lacked clitic doubling entirely was always hard to reconcile with the existence of (52), which is possible without right-dislocation intonation.[21]

(52) Jean lui   a   parlé   à elle.
     Jean her$_{DAT}$ has spoken to her

An additional reason for thinking that clitic doubling in (49) and (50) constitutes a single phenomenon comes from Jaeggli's (1986, p. 24) observation that in Spanish dative clitic doubling is sometimes obligatory, in particular in inalienable possession constructions.

(53) Le   examinaron   los dientes al   caballo.
      it$_{DAT}$ they-examined the teeth   to-the horse

(54) *Examinaron los dientes al caballo.

Having taken clitic doubling in right-dislocation to be the same phenomenon as standard clitic doubling, we are now in a position to link this Spanish contrast to the following French one (see Kayne 1975, sec. 2.14):

(55) Une pierre lui   est tombée sur la tête, à Jean.
     a   stone him$_{DAT}$ is fallen   on the head to Jean

(56) *Une pierre est tombée sur la tête à Jean.

Doubling is obligatory here in French;[22] the fact that (55) requires dislocation intonation on à Jean is now an independent fact.

The question that we are now ready to ask is this: what is the syntactic status of the right-dislocated phrase? I would like to make the following proposal. The right-dislocated phrase in (45)–(47), (50), and (55) is in complement position. It is not right-adjoined to anything, any more than a normal complement is. Thus, right-dislocation constructions are perfectly compatible with the general claim that I have made concerning the systematic unavailability of right-adjunction.

Taking right-dislocated phrases to be in complement position, rather than right-adjoined to VP or IP, provides an immediate answer to the question raised by the fact that right-dislocation is "upward-bounded."

(57)   Que Jean lui   ait parlé, à Marie m'attriste.
       that Jean her$_{DAT}$ has spoken to Marie me makes-sad

(58)   *Que Jean lui ait parlé m'attriste, à Marie.

The strong ungrammaticality of (58) is now expected. In the absence of right-adjunction, *à Marie* can occur in the matrix sentence only as a complement of the matrix verb *attrister*, but that leads to a theta-violation.[23]

The unavailability of right-adjunction leads me, of course, to take a similar position with respect to Spanish clitic doubling of the nondislocated sort. The lexical DP must be a complement. The conclusion is, then, that the Italian examples (49) and (50) both have clitic doubling and both have the phrase *a suo fratello* in complement position. One question remains: how is the difference between (49) and (50) to be expressed?

The answer, I think, lies in considering the construction that Cinque (1990, chap. 2) calls clitic left-dislocation (CLLD).

(59)   A suo fratello, glielo   dico subito.
       to his brother him$_{DAT}$ + it I-say right-away

This resembles right-dislocation in displaying clitic doubling, while differing from it in that the doubled phrase is not in complement position but in a left-hand position higher than subject position. Now Raffaella Zanuttini (personal communication) notes that she finds left-dislocation with clitic doubling of a dative, as in (59), better when there is an accusative clitic in addition to the dative clitic. This ameliorating effect (for her) of the accusative clitic recalls Cinque's observation mentioned above for (49) and leads one to wonder if CLLD and right-dislocation/clitic doubling are not to be more closely related than in Cinque 1990 (even if sensitivity to the accusative clitic in (59) is limited to some speakers).

Let me suggest, in fact, that CLLD be derived by movement of the left-dislocated phrase from complement position (a possibility anticipated by Dobrovie-Sorin (1990, p. 394)). Thus, *a suo fratello* in (59) originates in complement position and moves leftward to its surface position. If correct, this provides a straightforward account of the fact that CLLD displays sensitivity to strong islands (Cinque 1990, p. 59).[24]

One reason that Cinque (p. 60) did not adopt a movement analysis is that Italian clitic doubling is more pervasive in CLLD sentences than elsewhere. From a standard perspective, accusative clitic doubling is in fact totally unavailable except with CLLD.

(60) Il   vino, lo porto   subito.
      the wine it I-bring right-away

(61) *Lo porto subito il vino.

This makes deriving (60) from a structure resembling (61) seem implausible. However, by prohibiting right-adjunction, the present theory has forced us to analyze right-dislocation as having the dislocated phrase in complement position, so that (62) becomes an instance of clitic doubling.

(62) Lo porto subito, il vino.

Consequently, to derive (60) by leftward movement of *il vino* from complement position is perfectly plausible.

The importance of CLLD for the present discussion may not be evident, since Cinque's base-generation analysis of (60) is not incompatible with the LCA. The point is rather that if we adopt a movement analysis of (60), as I am proposing, then we have the possibility of distinguishing (61) from (62), and (49) from (50), which I repeat here.

(63) Glielo   dico a suo fratello.
      him$_{DAT}$ + it I-say to his brother

(64) Glielo dico, a suo fratello.

Given a movement analysis of CLLD, we can treat right-dislocation as an instance of CLLD at LF, by taking (62) and (64) to involve leftward movement at LF of *il vino* and *a suo fratello* to the same landing site that they overtly occupy in (60) and (59).[25]

The difference between (63) and (64), from this perspective, is that only the latter involves CLLD at LF. The former need not involve any LF movement of *a suo fratello*.[26] Note that CLLD at LF implies dislocation intonation. This could be expressed by having an optional feature present in the "overt syntax" that would feed both LF (triggering CLLD-type movement) and PF (triggering a certain intonation contour).

The fact that French allows the equivalent of (64), but not the equivalent of (63), can be stated by saying that (at least in French) (65) holds.

(65) No clitic can asymmetrically c-command the corresponding doubled lexical phrase at LF.

This will carry over to accusative doubling.[27]

(66) *Jean la   voit Marie.
    Jean her sees Marie

(67) Jean la voit, Marie.

(68) Marie, Jean la voit.

In (66) the clitic does asymmetrically c-command *Marie*, and the sentence is consequently ungrammatical. In (68) it does not, as a result of overt syntactic movement. In (67) it does not, as a result of LF movement.

In Italian (in some cases) and in Spanish quite generally, a dative clitic is permitted to asymmetrically c-command the doubled phrase at LF, thereby allowing (counterparts to) (63).[28] In peninsular Spanish accusative clitics act like the French ones in (66)–(68). An independent property of Spanish is responsible for the appearance of the preposition *a* before *María*.[29]

(69) *Juan la ve a María.

(70) Juan la ve, a María.

(71) A María, Juan la ve.

In conclusion, then, Romance right-dislocation does not involve right-adjunction. The right-dislocated phrase is in complement position. It differs from an ordinary complement in that it undergoes LF movement of the CLLD type.

Chapter 8

Relatives and Possessives

8.1 Postnominal Possessives in English

In (1) the phrase *of John's* is not plausibly a complement of *picture*.

(1) I have two pictures of John's.

(In fact, it can cooccur with a true complement of *picture*, as in *two pictures of Mary of John's*.) Nor can *of John's* in (1) be taken to be adjoined to some projection of N, since right-adjunction is illicit. In Kayne 1993 I proposed an analysis of this construction that is compatible with the LCA, based in part on Szabolcsi's (1981; 1983; to appear) analysis of Hungarian possessives.

Like English possessors, Hungarian possessors are prenominal. They can be in nominative Case, and when they are, they are preceded by the definite article; that is, Hungarian has the near equivalent of (*)*the John's two pictures*. I argued in Kayne 1993 that it is advantageous to take English to have a phonetically unrealized counterpart to the Hungarian D^0, in other words, that *John's two pictures* has the structure (2) (see the discussion of (30) of chapter 3).

(2) D^0 [John ['s [two pictures]]]

Szabolcsi argues strongly that Hungarian also has a (phonetically unrealized) indefinite D^0 that can precede the possessor phrase; however, in that case the possessor must move into the specifier of that D^0, where it picks up dative Case, and then out of the DP entirely.

I interpret this obligatory movement in terms of Case. In (2) the definite D^0 plays a role in the Case licensing of the possessor *John*; that is, *'s* is not sufficient (and neither is possessive Agr in Hungarian).[1] However, indefinite D^0 is not a Case licenser. This has the consequence in Hungarian of forcing the possesor to move up past D^0 to a valid Case-licensing position. English does not have the possibility of legitimizing dative Case in Spec,DP but can use another strategy, that of moving the NP (perhaps QP) *two pictures* to Spec,DP and inserting the preposition *of* in D^0.

(3) [two pictures]$_i$ [[$_D$ of] [John ['s [e]$_i$]]]

This turns D^0 into a Case licenser and "rescues" the structure.

I assume numerals like *two*, quantifiers like *every, many, some, any*, and also the article $a(n)^2$ to be generable within the NP/QP below *'s*. (Some of these cannot actually occur overtly below *'s* in English: for example, **John's some pictures*, although the equivalent is possible in Hungarian.)[3] On the other hand, I take English *the* to be uniquely a D^0, that is, not to be generable below *'s* (and I assume that the complement of *'s* cannot be DP). This implies that (3) can have no counterpart with *the* replacing *two*, and it thereby contributes to an account of the ungrammaticality of (4).[4]

(4) *?I found the pictures of John's/his.

This account of (4) needs to be fleshed out a bit more, as shown by (5).

(5) *?I found the two pictures of John's/his.

In addition to accounting for the fact that *the* cannot occur in the position of *two* in (3), we must make certain that *the* cannot take the phrase shown in (3) as its complement. For this, I will simply take as given that *the* cannot have a DP complement.[5]

8.2 Relative Clauses in English

The question now arises why (6) is fully grammatical.

(6) I found the (two) pictures of John's/his that you lent me.

I will propose that in (6) *the (two) pictures of John's/his* is actually not a constituent, contrary to the case of (4) and (5). Instead, *(two) pictures of John's/his that you lent me* is a constituent distinct from *the*. The category of that constituent clearly cannot be DP in (6), given what has just been said about (5). More generally put, it must be the case that *the*, although it cannot have, say, *(two) pictures of John's* as its complement, can have as its complement *(two) pictures of John's that you lent me*.

The only conceivable way that could be true is if the head of the phrase (*two*) *pictures of John's that you lent me* is not present in (*two*) *pictures of John's*. This in turn suggests directly that the head of the former is the complementizer *that*, in other words, that that phrase is a CP. For it to be a CP with *that* as its head, it must be the case that that CP contains (*two*) *pictures of John's* in its specifier. The most natural conclusion is then that that phrase appears in Spec,CP as the result of movement.

(7) [(two) pictures of John's]$_i$ [that [... me [e]$_i$]]

In other words, we have reached the conclusion that the raising/ promotion analysis of restrictive relative clauses developed by Vergnaud (1974) must be basically correct.[6]

If we adopt the approach to reconstruction put forth by Chomsky (1993), we are led to the raising analysis of relatives for a second reason, given the ambiguity (comparable to the ambiguity in Chomsky's interrogative examples) with respect to the antecedent of the reflexive in (8).

(8) John bought the picture of himself that Bill saw.

The raising analysis of relatives provides a direct answer to the question of where relative clauses are attached. They are not plausibly complements of N, nor, from my perspective, can they be right-adjoined to N or to any projection of N (or D), for the simple reason that right-adjunction is banned in general. Instead, the raising analysis says that the relative clause in (8) is a complement of D (*the*): '[$_{DP}$ D^0 CP]'.[7] This structure is in fact the only one of those that have been proposed for relative clauses that is compatible with the present LCA-based theory.

Vergnaud's (1974) analysis has in common with that of Smith (1969) the idea that the relative clause is moved past the "head" of the relative (*picture of himself* in (8)) from a postdeterminer position. I am proposing that although the determiner and relative clause form a constituent, relatives lack any "head" position (apart from D^0) outside the relative CP.

(9) the [picture of himself [that [Bill saw [e]]]]

The empty category in object position is bound by the phrase *picture of himself*, which has raised to Spec,CP. *Picture of himself* here is a phrase probably of category NP. The fact that the phrase in question contains an overt complement is not fundamental to the construction; that is, (10) will have an exactly parallel representation.

(10) the [[$_{NP}$ picture] [that [Bill saw [e]]]]

In some languages, for example, Romanian, the head noun of the NP in Spec,CP will raise out of CP and left-adjoin to D^0.[8]

(11) cartea   pe care   am   citit-o
      book-the *pe* which I-have read it

For English and similar languages, on the other hand, there seems to be no reason to postulate any more movement in the overt syntax than indicated in (10).[9]

The Romanian example (11) contains a relative pronoun. Relative pronouns appear to pose a problem, since if *picture* is in Spec,CP in (10), where is the relative pronoun in (12)?

(12) a. the picture which Bill saw
      b. the person who Bill saw

That is, the "head" of the relative and the relative pronoun appear to be competing for the same position.

Valentina Bianchi (personal communication) has pointed out that this tension should actually provide an account of the fact that (French and) Italian relative pronouns are generally impossible in the equivalent of (12).

(13) *la persona cui Bill ha visto
       the person   who Bill has seen

(14) la persona con cui   Bill ha parlato
      the person   with whom Bill has spoken

Italian *cui* is impossible as a direct object relative pronoun, but possible as a prepositional object,[10] and the same holds of French *qui* in "headed" relative clauses.

(15) *la personne qui Bill a vue (same as (13))

(16) la personne avec qui Bill a parlé (same as (14))

An approach to (15)–(16) in terms of obligatory deletion of the relative pronoun was suggested in Kayne 1976. Thinking of Chomsky's (1981, p. 65) "avoid pronoun," this might be reformulated in contemporary terms as "avoid relative pronoun if possible" (in French and Italian; the grammatical relatives corresponding to (13) and (15) have the complementizer *che/que*). But certain French facts discussed in Kayne 1976, p. 261, cast doubt on this idea.[11]

(17) *l'homme la femme de qui tu as insulteé
     the man the wife of who you have insulted

(18) l'homme avec la femme de qui tu t'es disputé
     the man with the wife of who you REFL-is argued
     'the man with whose wife you argued'

These show the same contrast as the previous pair (i.e., sensitivity to the presence of a preposition) yet do not readily lend themselves to an "avoid relative pronoun if possible" perspective.

I will pursue a different approach, one that incorporates Bianchi's suggestion, as follows: in French and Italian the structures in (13), (15), and (17) are ungrammatical because once *cui, qui,* and *la femme de qui* have filled Spec,CP, there is no "room" for *persona, personne* or *homme*. There is extra "room" in (14), (16), and (18) because the preposition in those examples provides it, namely, by making its specifier position available.

I begin by proposing that relative pronouns originate as determiners that are split off from their associated NP by movement of the latter.

(19) the [C^0 [he broke it with which hammer]]

Wh-movement of the PP to Spec,CP yields the structure in (20).

(20) the [with which hammer [C^0 [he broke it [e]]]]

The NP *hammer* then raises to Spec,PP (probably via Spec,*which*).

(21) the [$_{CP}$ [$_{PP}$ hammer$_i$ [with which [e]$_i$]] [C^0 ...

The plausibility of having an underlying constituent *which hammer* here is clear. I take *who* to have a similar status, despite the absence of **who man*,[12] and the same for Italian/French *cui/qui*. Thus, (16) will start out as (22).

(22) la [C^0 [Bill a parlé avec qui personne]]

Wh-movement of PP will yield (23).

(23) la [avec qui personne [C^0 [...

Raising of *personne* to Spec,PP proceeds as in (21).

(24) la [$_{CP}$ [$_{PP}$ personne$_i$ [avec qui [e]$_i$]] [C^0 ...

The contrasts found in (13)–(18) can now be accounted for in terms of the landing site for the NPs *persona, personne,* and *homme*. When the constituent moved to Spec,CP is headed by a preposition, those NPs can raise to the specifier of that preposition. When, in French and Italian, no preposition is present, those NPs have no available landing site, and the result is therefore an ill-formed relative clause structure.

(25) *la [qui personne [C^0 ...

More precisely, the reason must be that a well-formed "headed" restrictive relative clause structure requires that *personne* reach in the overt syntax a position governed by D^0.[13]

The idea that the contrasts found in (13)–(18) depend on the availability of a Spec,PP is likely to be supported by what I take to be parallel contrasts found with reciprocals, in French and Italian. For example, in the latter:[14]

(26) *Hanno   visto l'uno   l'altro.
      they-have seen the one the other

(27) Hanno   parlato l'uno   con l'altro.
      they-have spoken the one with the other

In (27) *l'uno* is arguably in Spec,PP (this is very close, modulo the LCA, to Belletti's (1982, p. 104) proposal that it is adjoined to PP). The idea would then be to say that (26) is ungrammatical because it contains no comparably adequate position for *l'uno*.

Although *personne* in (25) has no position that it can be successfully raised to, the same does not hold of corresponding English cases. For example:

(28) the [which picture [C^0 ...

The contrast between English, on the one hand, and French and Italian, on the other, can be stated by allowing English to use the specifier position of the *wh*-determiner itself as a landing site. That is, (28) becomes (29).[15]

(29) the [$_{CP}$ [$_{DP}$ picture$_i$ [which [e]$_i$]] [C^0 ...

(At present I have no account of why French and Italian differ from English in this respect.)

Essentially similar to (29), apart from the extra embedding, is (30).

(30) the [$_{CP}$ [[$_{DP}$ man$_i$ [who [e]$_i$]]'s wife] [C^0 ...

Here, the phrase *who man's wife* is moved to Spec,CP and *man* is moved to the inner Spec,DP (D = *who*). In both (29) and (30) the NP (*picture/ man*) moves from the complement position of *which/who* to its specifier.

This kind of local movement is not sufficient to permit the following (even allowing for the additional movement across a preposition seen in (21) and (24)):

(31) the book the author of which I know personally

In this sort of example *book* must raise from the complement position of *which* up to Spec,*the* (and remain there). This longer movement of the relativized NP (*book*) is possible in English but absent in many other Germanic languages (see Webelhuth 1992, p. 129), for reasons that are unclear.

Still longer movement is necessary in relatives like (32).

(32) ??the man the possibility of you marrying whom became a reality
        only yesterday

Here, the NP *man* must raise from the post-*whom* position to the specifier of the second *the*. The movement approach I am pursuing makes sense of the contrast with (33).

(33) *the man the possibility of who(m) marrying you became a reality
        only yesterday

The reason is that (33) involves extraction of *man* from within the subject of *marrying*, as opposed to from within the object, as in (32). Thus, the status of (33) has the familiar character of a subject island movement violation (whatever the optimal formulation of that is).[16]

Summing up this section so far, the raising/promotion analysis of relatives, which is by far the most natural analysis of relatives from an LCA perspective,[17] has led me to propose that both *the book that I read* and *the book which I read* involve movement to the specifier of the CP that is sister to $D = the$. In the first case, what is moved is just the NP *book*; in the second, what is moved to Spec,CP is the phrase *which book*. Further movement then takes place within *which book*, yielding *book which [e]*. In standard English the complementizer *that* cannot appear in the second type of relative.

(34) *the book which that I read

This is generally thought of in terms of an incompatibility between an overtly filled Spec,CP and an overtly filled C^0. However, under my proposal for *the book that I read*, that kind of relative violates the "Doubly Filled Comp Filter," unless that filter is now specified to see phrases in Spec,CP only when they are *wh*-phrases.[18]

As for relatives like *the book John read*, I follow the standard view that they differ from *the book that John read* only in having a null C^0. This small difference, combined with the idea that *book* is in Spec,CP, has an interesting effect.

(35) I just read the book about your ancestors ?(that) your son
       published last year.

When the NP moved to Spec,CP (here *book about your ancestors*) contains a complement, the zero complementizer yields less than full acceptability. This effect is very sharp when the NP moved to Spec,CP contains a relative itself.[19]

(36) I just read the book that's about your ancestors *(that) your son
       gave me last year.

Here it is *book that's about your ancestors* that has been moved to the Spec,CP position following *the* from the complement position following *me*. This so-called stacked relative structure is fine when the complementizer of the less embedded relative is *that*, but impossible if it is null.[20] The idea that *book (that's) about your ancestors* is in Spec,CP makes it possible to relate these restrictions to those discussed by Emonds (1976, p. 19); his "surface recursion restriction" translates in my terms into the generalization that, in a number of cases, a phrase (with)in a specifier position cannot have an overt complement (of a certain sort).[21] This seems to hold of Spec,CP when relative C^0 is null, though not when it is nonnull, for reasons that are unclear.

8.3 N-Final Relative Clauses

Relative clauses in English and similar languages can be thought of as N-initial if one focuses on the CP that is sister to D^0. If the analysis sketched above is correct, then English relative clauses become N-initial only as a result of leftward movement. In *the picture of John that I showed you* the noun *picture* becomes initial in CP as a result of the phrase *picture of John* moving to Spec,CP. In *the picture of John which I showed you*, what moves to Spec,CP is the phrase *which picture of John*. The noun *picture* becomes initial in CP as a result of movement of *picture of John* to Spec,*which*P.

Many languages have relative clause structures in which the noun follows the relative clause. In an LCA-based theory, these are predicted to have different properties from relative clauses of the N-initial sort.

The basic reason is that the N cannot come to be final in a way that mimics the way in which N comes to be initial in English relatives. In English N reaches initial position within CP as a result of movement of the NP containing it to Spec,CP in *that*-relatives, and as a result of movement of NP to Spec,*wh*P (in addition to movement to Spec,CP) in *which*-relatives. But specifier positions are always on the left (since specifiers are an instance of adjunction and since adjunction is always left-adjunction), no matter what the language. Therefore, the final position of N in relative structures in languages like Japanese cannot be attributed to movement of NP to Spec,CP (or any other specifier).

I will first consider two ways in which the N-final relative clause structure of languages like Japanese differs from the N-initial one of languages like English.[22]

(37) a. N-final relatives lack relative pronouns.

b. N-final relatives never display a complementizer that is identical to the normal complementizer of sentential complementation.

I will attempt to account for these two asymmetries in a maximally parsimonious way, namely, by showing that they essentially follow from the word order difference itself, given the LCA. (Under the standard assumption that word order can vary independently of hierarchical structure, it would be impossible to achieve this strong a result.)

The question of (37) is related to the question of how similar N-initial and N-final relatives are. To try to derive (37) from the word order difference alone amounts to taking the position that apart from that difference, the two types of relative clause construction are essentially identical. If that is so, then N-final relatives must involve the same 'D^0 CP' structure that N-initial relatives have.

Now many N-final languages lack any equivalent of English *the*, so that the D^0 will not be visible. Of those that do have a visible D^0, I will focus on Amharic as described by Gragg (1972), and I will take that language to provide a significant clue to the syntax of D^0 in N-final relatives. In Amharic the relative clause (which is V-final) precedes the definite article, which itself precedes the N. This suggests that the relative clause has moved into Spec,DP. However, if starting from 'D^0 CP' the entire CP moved to Spec,DP, then we would not expect N to follow D.[23] I conclude that the relative clause that precedes the definite article in Amharic is not CP.

Rather, the pre-D relative clause must be a projection smaller than CP; let us call it IP (abstracting away from the question of Tense vs. Agreement). The movement of IP to Spec,DP provides a way of obtaining a post-D noun, namely, by having IP-movement strand in Spec,CP the same NP that moves to Spec,CP in N-initial languages. Recall the structure given for English relatives above.

(38) the [[$_{NP}$ picture] [that [Bill saw [e]]]]

Here the NP *picture* has moved to Spec,CP, leaving a trace in object position. Simplifying this representation, we have (39).

(39) the [[$_{NP}$ picture] [that IP]]

Moving IP to Spec,DP yields (40).

(40) IP$_j$ [the [[$_{NP}$ picture] [that [e]$_j$]]]

This corresponds to the observed structure in Amharic, except for the presence of *that*. Assume, then, that the relative clause configuration in Amharic is really closer to those English relatives that have a phonetically unrealized C^0.

(41) IP$_j$ [the [[$_{NP}$ picture] [C^0 [e]$_j$]]]

This is what I take to be the structure of the Amharic construction in question.[24] What is usually called the relative clause is the IP that has been raised to Spec,DP, stranding a zero complementizer (and also stranding NP in Spec,CP).[25] (The fact that C^0 must be empty recalls the *that*-trace effect in English, though I will leave open the question of exactly how to exclude (40).) Generalizing from (41), N-final relative structures with no overt D^0 will have the representation (42), with D^0 and C^0 both empty.

(42) IP$_j$ [D^0 [[$_{NP}$ picture] [C^0 [e]$_j$]]]

Summing up so far, I started by assuming that UG makes available for relativization a 'D^0 CP' structure,[26] where CP is the complement of D^0. UG prohibits the existence of the mirror-image complement-head structure '*CP D^0' and leads us instead to (42) as the correct representation for relativization structures where the relative clause precedes N.[27] The fact that such relative clauses must be IPs now provides an explanation for (37b).

Pre-N relative clauses cannot display the normal C^0 of sentential complementation because they are necessarily IPs, and cannot be CPs. (The pre-N relative IP originates within a CP, but that CP must have a null C^0, which in any case follows N.) In English-type relativization structures, the corresponding IP remains in situ, so that C^0 can be overt and can be identical to the normal sentential complementizer. (Left open is the question of why in N-initial relatives the overt relative C^0 is sometimes identical (e.g., English, French, Italian, Spanish) and sometimes not (e.g., the Scandinavian languages) to the C^0 of sentential complementation.)

The fact that the preposed relative in (42) is of category IP rather than CP appears to provide at least a partial account of another cross-linguistic generalization noted by Keenan (1985, p. 160), namely, that with few exceptions the verbs of prenominal relatives are nonfinite/participial, having reduced tense possibilities as compared with finite verbs. On the other hand, relatives with fully finite verbs are common in postnominal relatives. This would follow if full finiteness is normally incompatible with IP being split off from C^0, as if, for example, finiteness required incorporation of I^0 to C^0 in the overt syntax (i.e., before LF/PF) and that relation could not be reconstructed subsequent to overt movement of IP away from C^0.[28]

Now consider *wh*-relatives in English.

(43) the $[_{CP} [_{DP}$ picture$_i$ [which [e]$_i$]] $[C^0 \ldots$

In these constructions what moves to Spec,CP is the DP *which picture*. Within that DP the NP *picture* moves to Spec,*which*. To mimic this in an N-final structure—that is, to get N to be final and to do so in a way parallel to the derivation of (42)—one would have to move everything following *picture* to Spec,*the*. But the material following *picture* in (43) is not a constituent, and such a derivation is therefore precluded. (IP-movement to Spec,DP might be possible but would not yield an N-final structure.)[29] Thus, the presence of a *wh*-word in addition to the NP *picture* turns out to be incompatible with having N be final. Put another way, N-final relativization does not admit the presence of a relative pronoun. Hence, we have succeeded in deriving (37a).

A further striking difference between N-initial and N-final relative structures is discussed by Cole (1987): internally headed relatives are found only where one would expect the latter, namely, in languages that are at least partially head-final. Cole proposes that internally headed relatives actually have a null anaphoric "head" and that the limitation to head-final structures is due to the general condition that an anaphor must not both precede and c-command its antecedent (which the anaphoric head would do in an N-initial language). I agree with Cole that there is a null "head" and also that the limitation to N-final structures is due to a c-command violation. However, Cole specifically argues for a formulation mentioning both c-command and precedence. If I am correct in taking left-hand relative clauses to be left-adjoined higher than N (as forced by the LCA), there is no longer any need to mention precedence, since the left-hand relative is not c-commanded by the (null) "head," whereas the right-hand relative in languages like English would be.

I would like to briefly suggest an analysis of internally headed relatives slightly different from Cole's, as follows. Recall the analysis proposed above for N-final relativization.

(44) $IP_j [D^0 [_{CP} [_{NP} picture] [C^0 [e]_j]]]$

Starting from a 'D CP' structure, the NP *picture* is moved to Spec,CP and then the IP complement of the empty C^0 is moved to Spec,DP. That IP contains the trace of *picture*.

(45) $[_{IP} \ldots [e]_i \ldots] [D^0 [_{CP} [_{NP} picture]_i [C^0 \ldots$

Assume, however, that Chomsky (1993) is correct in proposing that a trace is actually a copy of the moved constituent. Then the relevant part of (44)/(45) is more exactly (46) (prior to PF deletion).

(46) $[_{IP} \ldots [picture]_i \ldots] [D^0 [_{CP} [_{NP} picture]_i [C^0 \ldots$

My proposal now is that internally headed relatives are identical to (45)/(46) except that instead of the first instance of *picture* being deleted, as in (45), it is the second that is deleted.

(47) $[_{IP} \ldots [picture]_i \ldots] [D^0 [_{CP} [_{NP} e]_i [C^0 \ldots$

From this perspective, the reason that N-initial relativization of the English type has no internally headed counterpart could be largely as Cole proposes. The English structure is (48).

(48) $D^0 [_{CP} [_{NP} picture]_i [C^0 [_{IP} \ldots [e]_i \ldots$

An internally headed counterpart would have to delete (at PF) the first instance of *picture* instead of the second.

(49) $*D^0 [_{CP} [_{NP} e]_i [C^0 [_{IP} \ldots [picture]_i \ldots$

This will be excluded if we adopt (50).

(50) A given chain link c_k can license PF deletion of another link c_l of the same chain only if c_l does not c-command c_k.

(In (46) neither the first nor the second instance of *picture* c-commands the other, so there are two possible outcomes, (45) and (47).)[30]

It is to be noted that (50) also covers the classical cases of lowering violations (see Fiengo 1977).

8.4   Reduced Relatives and Adjectives

At the beginning of section 8.2 I discussed contrasts like the following:

(51)   *?We were admiring the sweater of his.

(52)   We were admiring the sweater of his that was lying on the sofa.

The contrast was attributed in part to the fact that in (52) *sweater of his* does not originate in the post-*the* position but rather moves there (i.e., to Spec,CP) from within the relative IP. Now consider (53).

(53)   (?)We were admiring the (one) sweater of his given to him by his
          wife.

(53) seems to have much more the status of (52) than that of (51), suggesting that it has some property or properties significantly in common with the former. On the other hand, (53) allows neither an overt complementizer nor a *wh*-phrase:

(54)   *the sweater of John's that/which given to him by . . .

This might suggest that what follows *the* in (53) is IP, and not CP. However, Vergnaud (1974, pp. 173ff.) has noted one respect in which these 'reduced' relatives exhibit the behavior of ordinary relatives.

(55)   I just read the book that you told me about *(that) your son gave
          me last year.

(56)   I just read the book that you told me about *?(that was) given to
          me by your son last year.

When relatives are "stacked," the second one can neither have a zero complementizer nor be "reduced." These two restrictions could be unified if the latter involved a zero complementizer, too.

Let us therefore consider the following analysis, for a simple case like *the book sent to me*:

(57)   the $[_{CP}$ book$_i$ $[C^0$ $[_{IP}$ $[e]_i$ sent to me

The participial IP is embedded in a CP (see Kayne 1993; Mouchaweh

1985). (56) is deviant as a reduced relative because Spec,CP contains too complex an NP (*book that you told me about*) for an empty C^0, as in the discussion of (36). (53) is acceptable because *the* has a CP complement, as in (52) (and unlike the case of (51), where the complement of *the* is a DP). The impossibility of *that* in (57) might be reducible to a *that*-trace effect.[31]

The impossibility of *which* in (58) might have to do with Case.

(58) *the [$_{CP}$ [book$_i$ which [e]$_i$]$_j$ [C^0 [$_{IP}$ [e]$_j$ sent ...

Assume that *book* in both (57) and (58) receives Case through a (n incorporation) relation with *the* (recall the discussion of (11)) and further that Case on *book* is sufficient to license its trace in (57).[32] The empty category in Spec,IP in (58), on the other hand, is not the trace of *book*, and so plausibly cannot be licensed in the same way, or in any other way, whence the violation.

Lack of Case on the Spec,IP position is also a plausible reason for the impossibility of reduced relatives like the following, though more will need to be said about the fact that PRO in that position is not possible either:[33]

(59) *the book John fond of

Now consider (57) again, but this time with *book* not raised to Spec,CP and with I^0 and a lower trace indicated.

(60) the [$_{CP}$[C^0 [$_{IP}$[book]$_i$ [I^0 [$_{XP}$[e]$_i$ sent to me

If nothing further happens overtly, this derivation is presumably ruled out because Spec,CP is not filled (see note 30). Assume, however, that in (60) abstract incorporation of *book* to *the* is possible via C^0, so that *book* poses no Case problem. Then let us move XP to Spec,CP, eliminating the potential violation based on an unfilled Spec,CP.

(61) the [$_{CP}$ XP$_j$ [C^0 [$_{IP}$[book] [I^0 [e]$_j$

This structure corresponds to the ungrammatical (62).

(62) *the sent to me book

Arguably, (62) violates the same constraint as (55)/(56), namely, that the specifier of the empty complementizer is filled by a phrase (*sent to me*) whose head (*sent*) has an overt complement (*to me*). If we replace *sent to me* by a comparable phrase with no overt complement (but with some material to the left of the head), then this violation disappears.

(63) the recently sent book

(Compare *the recently arrived letter, the much referred to hypothesis, the little slept in bed.*)[34]

Thus, examples like (63) are seen to be a subtype of relative clause structure with preposing, in particular insofar as they are derived from the same kind of underlying structure (60) as ordinary relative clauses. Note that in that case there is no need to take pseudopassives like (*much*) *referred to* or (*little*) *slept in* to be lexical items.[35]

In languages like German the construction exemplified in (63) is more productive than in English, allowing cases like *the by John recently sent book*. I take the German construction to be parallel to the English one (i.e., to involve (60)/(61)), with the independently needed difference that XP in German can contain complements to the left of participial V (these complements must have been moved to intermediate specifier positions), just as V in German can normally end up being preceded by complements in a way not available in English.

The idea that (63) is a relative clause structure of the form 'D⁰ CP' is supported by the following contrast, parallel to that between (51) and (53):

(64) *?The sweater of John's is beautiful.

(65) ?The recently arrived sweater of John's is beautiful.

An obvious question is whether prenominal adjectives ever display the same behavior as these prenominal participial phrases.

(66) ?The yellow sweater of John's is beautiful.

This sentence seems to me to be close in status to the participial example, especially if the adjective is stressed.[36] This suggests a representation with a CP complement of *the*.

(67) the $[_{CP} [_{XP}[e]_i$ yellow$]_j$ $[C^0 [_{IP}$[sweater of John's$]_i$ $[I^0 [e]_j$

Sweater of John's$_i$ is in Spec,IP. The complement of I^0, '$[_{XP} [e]_i$ yellow$]_j$,' has been moved to Spec,CP.

I have claimed that *the book recently sent to me* and *the recently sent book* are essentially similar except that the latter involves the preposing of *recently sent* to the specifier position of the CP sister to *the*.[37] I have also suggested that some (stressed) prenominal adjectives can follow the same kind of derivation, as in *the yellow sweater of John's*, that is, that (stressed) *yellow* can be preposed to Spec,CP from its original position following *sweater of John's* (which is in Spec,IP). This leads to the question of the unacceptability (even with stress) of (68).

(68) *The sweater of John's yellow is really beautiful.

Although I have no explanation for the fact that simple adjectives cannot remain postnominal (i.e., post-DP, with DP = *sweater of John's* contained in Spec,IP; see (57)) in the way that participial phrases can (see Chomsky 1981, p. 166), it is of interest to mention a case in French that shows a parallel difference between simple adjectives and participials (see Ronat 1977).

(69)   celui envoyé à Jean
       celui sent   to Jean

(70) *celui jaune
       celui yellow

Celui seems to be bimorphemic, with *ce* the demonstrative root and *lui* a pronoun. It would normally be translated as 'the one'. It can be followed by a full relative (*celui qui a été envoyé à Jean* 'the one that has been sent to Jean') and by a reduced participial relative, but not by a simple adjective.

   If I am correct in interpreting (70) to indicate that the prohibition seen in English (68) is valid for French, too, it is surprising that French allows (71).

(71) le   livre jaune
      the book yellow

A solution is proposed and justified by Cinque (1993b), as follows. There are two quite different sources for adnominal adjectives. In addition to the "reduced relative" source that I have been discussing,[38] APs can be generated in specifier positions (of various functional heads that occur) between D and N.

   As Cinque argues, and as argued by others whom he cites, (71) is an instance of an AP generated above N. The observed order in (71) is due to the N having raised past the AP to a higher functional head (which is lower than D).

   It should be noted, however, that the idea of invoking N-raising as a means of accounting for the French/English contrast that holds for (71) is independent of the idea of base-generating *jaune/yellow* in a specifier position between D and N. Let F be one of the functional heads intervening between D and N under that analysis, and consider again (61), repeated in essence here.

(72) the $[_{CP}[_{XP}$ yellow$_j]$ $[C^0[_{IP}[$book$]$ $[I^0$ $[e]_j$

We have seen reason to take English to allow XP to be an adjective phrase (preposed from the predicate position within IP), as indicated. The French counterpart would be (73).

(73) le $[_{CP}[_{XP}$ jaune$_j]$ $[C^0$ $[_{IP}[$livre$]$ $[I^0$ $[e]_j$

Adding F below D but above CP yields (74).

(74) le $[_{FP}$ F^0 $[_{CP}$ $[_{XP}$ jaune$_j]$ $[C^0$ $[_{IP}[$livre$]$ $[I^0$ $[e]_j$

Assume that *livre*, the head of the phrase in Spec,IP, can raise overtly in French to C^0 [39] and then raise again to F^0. Then we can derive (71) by N-raising without needing to have two separate sources for adjectives like *yellow/jaune*.

All such APs will originate in predicate position and prepose to their subject NP by moving to Spec,CP. No further overt movement is necessary for English *the yellow book*, just as no further movement is needed for *the recently arrived book*. In French N-raising will apply to the corresponding structure in (74), to yield the observed *le livre jaune*.[40]

8.5   More on Possessives

Returning to (70), we might now say that *celui* is not an N. Rather, it is an XP composed of *ce* + *lui*. The pronominal part *lui* can alternate with its plural and feminine (singular or plural) counterparts, yielding the following forms:

(75) ceux, celle, celles = ce + eux, ce + elle, ce + elles

But there can be no further material inside this XP, and in particular no Agr projection that would yield agreement on the demonstrative:

(76) *ces + eux, *cette + elle, *ces + elles

Presumably because of its internally defective character, *celui* and the like cannot be interpreted in "isolation"; that is, (77) is not possible.

(77) *Jean a   vu   celui.
     Jean has seen *celui*

The grammaticality of (69) (and similarly for the corresponding full relative) suggests that *celui* can only be interpreted in Spec,CP.

If so, then given *celui de Jean* '... of Jean', *celui-ci* '... here', we would be led to conclude that both *-ci* and the possessive *de Jean* (with *de* a prepositional complementizer, as indicated in (78)) involve a CP structure.[41]

(78) D^0 [$_{CP}$ celui$_j$ [de [$_{IP}$ Jean [I^0 [e]$_j$ ...

In standard French D^0 is necessarily empty with *celui*. More regular would be the following, with an overt D^0:

(79) la [$_{CP}$ voiture$_j$ [de [$_{IP}$ Jean [I^0 [e]$_j$ ...
      the   car   of   Jean

De here serves to Case-license *Jean*. The relation between *voiture* and *Jean* would presumably be established within IP.[42]

There is, however, a strong resemblance between the post-D^0 structure in (79) and the structure given in section 8.1 for English *two pictures of John's*.

(80) [two pictures]$_i$ [of [John ['s [e]$_i$ ...

There, I took *of* to have been inserted in D^0, and *two pictures* to be in Spec,DP. Even if the categorial difference between CP and DP is slight, as Szabolcsi (1992) argues, let me recast (79) so as to make it more explicitly a DP structure, using, however, the symbol D/P as in Kayne 1993 to represent a prepositional determiner *de* (comparable to a prepositional complementizer).[43]

(81) la [$_{D/PP}$ voiture$_j$ [de [$_{IP}$ Jean [I^0 [e]$_j$ ...

This requires restating the condition on *celui* to be that *celui* must occupy Spec,XP, where XP is sister (modulo the F of (74)) to some D^0 (*la* in (81)). And we can now take I^0 in (81) to be an abstract counterpart to English *'s*, making the possessive interpretation within IP more straightforward.

More specifically, I take the D/PP of (81) to be parallel to the D/PP that occurs as sister phrase to the abstract copula in (82).

(82) ... BE [$_{D/PP}$[D/P^0 [$_{IP}$ Jean [I^0 [voiture]$_j$ ...

As I argued in Kayne 1993, to a significant extent in agreement with Freeze (1992), this structure is what underlies (83).

(83) Jean a   une voiture.
     Jean has a   car

Jean, which could not be Case-licensed in Spec,IP in (82), moves from there to Spec,D/PP, and then on to Spec,BE. The second step is licensed by incorporation of D/P^0 to BE. D/P^0 + BE is spelled out as HAVE.[44]

On the other hand, in (81) *Jean* is Case-licensed in situ, and it is the "possessed" phrase *voiture* that raises to Spec,D/PP.

Although details remain to be filled in, this analysis succeeds in expressing the relation between *la voiture de Jean* and *Jean a une voiture* without having to derive the former from a full relative containing the verb *avoir* 'have'. Instead, the two share significant structure.

Despite not being or containing a full relative, the possessive structure in (81) is similar to a relative clause structure, with *de* corresponding to *that*.[45]

(84) la [$_{D/PP}$[$_{NP}$ voiture$_j$] [de [$_{IP}$ Jean [I^0 [e]$_j$ ...

(85) the [$_{CP}$[$_{NP}$ picture$_j$] [that [$_{IP}$ Bill saw [e]$_j$ ...

Now when the noun is not relational (i.e., not *sister*, etc.), English does not allow (84) at all with human possessors.[46]

(86) *the car of John, *the car of your older brother

Possible, on the other hand, is *the dreams of my youth*, where *my youth* is plausibly an inanimate possessor of *dreams*.

(87) the [$_{D/PP}$[$_{NP}$ dreams$_j$] [of [$_{IP}$ my youth I^0 [e]$_j$ ...

The parallelism between (87) and (85) allows a unified account of the following paradigm noted by Vergnaud (1974, p. 265):

(88) *the Paris

(89)   the Paris that I knew

(90)   the Paris of my youth

In English a proper name (of a city), like *Paris*, can normally not occur with *the*. The approach to relatives and possessives being developed here permits one to understand straightforwardly why the two constructions act alike in licensing *the*. (In a way somewhat similar to what was said above about French *celui*, the generalization could be stated (abstracting away from the F of (74)) by saying that a proper noun (NP) is prohibited in English from being the sister phrase to a definite article.)[47]

Though not a proper noun, English *ones* has a similar distribution.[48]

(91) *John remembers the ones.

(92)   John remembers the ones he had last night. ("dreams")

(93)   John remembers the ones of his youth.

Assuming essentially the same generalization that holds for proper nouns, the following contrast is of interest:

(94)   In this school, the students from New York are taller than the ones from New Jersey.

(95)   *In this school, the students of physics are taller than the ones of chemistry.

In discussing this kind of example, Jackendoff (1977, p. 59) suggests that the difference is due to the difference in hierarchical status between *from New Jersey* and *of chemistry*, the latter type being immediately dominated by N′, the former by N″. Furthermore, *one(s)* is incompatible with other material within N′. The different attachment levels are also reflected in relative ordering facts.

(96)   the students of chemistry from New Jersey

(97)   *the students from New Jersey of chemistry

Jackendoff's approach to (94)–(97), which does not cover (91), is not compatible with the present theory, which prohibits any structure of the following form, with the phrase *from New Jersey* taken either as a complement of N′ or as a phrase right-adjoined to N′:

(98)   *the $[_{N''}[_{N'}$ students of chemistry] [from New Jersey]]

The reason is that the phrase *from New Jersey* asymmetrically c-commands the subparts of the phrase *students of chemistry* and would therefore have to precede it, which it does not.

Instead, these facts should be looked at as follows. *Ones* is not allowed to head an NP sister to *the* (again abstracting away from the F^0 of (74)). This property, although itself in need of explanation, has the advantage (as compared with the idea that *ones* is incompatible with other material under N′) of excluding (91) and (95) simultaneously. (92)–(94) are admissible because they are all instances of the embedded CP or D/PP structure proposed above. For example:

(99)   the $[_{D/PP}[_{NP}$ ones$_i$] $[D/P^0$ $[_{IP}[e]_i$ I^0 [from New Jersey] . . .

Here the NP *ones* is not sister to *the*.

(96) also has the structure shown in (99), with the NP *ones* replaced by the NP *students of chemistry*. The ungrammaticality of (95) indicates that *of chemistry* can only be a complement of *student*, in other words, that it

cannot occur as a predicate, in the position of *from New Jersey* in (99). This suffices to account for (97), as well.[49]

Returning to possessives, I note that the difference between English *'s* and its abstract French counterpart is presumably what is responsible for the fact that French allows no Case licensing of the lexical possessor if the D/P^0 sister to IP remains empty.

(100)   John's car = $[D/P^0 \, [_{IP} \, John \, ['s \, [car]]]]$

(101)   *Jean voiture

When D/P is definite and *'s* is present in I^0, *John* can remain in situ. The combination of a definite but unrealized D/P with the abstract possessive I^0 of French does not suffice to allow *Jean* to do so. Another difference between French and English concerns the definite article.

(102)   la voiture de Jean

(103)   *?the car of John's

This could be due to some difference between *la* and *the*, and/or it could be attributed to *'s*. For example, it might be that *'s* must raise in LF to the D^0 occupied by *of* (which might be adjoined to D^0) and that an overt definite article does not admit a sister complement headed by *'s*.[50] (In *the car of John's that I most admire* the sister phrase of *the* is the CP headed by *that*.)

To conclude this section, the analysis given of *la voiture de Jean* and of *a car of John's* is straightforwardly compatible with the LCA and more specifically with my claim that UG countenances no right-adjunction at all. *De Jean* and *of John's* are not adjoined to *voiture/car*; instead, they are phrases (headed by *de/of*) whose specifier position contains *voiture/a car*. It is in this way that UG allows for possessive constructions of this sort.[51]

8.6   More on French *De*

The IP in (84), repeated here, expresses a possessive relation, with the possessed NP fronted to Spec,D/PP.

(104)   la $[_{D/PP}[_{NP} \, voiture_j]$ [de $[_{IP} \, Jean \, [I^0 \, [e]_j \, \ldots$

One might wonder if IP could in other instances—say, with an adjectival predicate, with the AP fronted—have the interpretation of a simple predication. The answer appears to be yes, at least in French.[52]

(105) le   rouge, de crayon
      the red   of pencil

(106) le [$_{D/PP}$[$_{AP}$ rouge$_j$] [de [$_{IP}$ crayon [I^0 [e]$_j$ ...

This is always pronounced with dislocation intonation (as indicated by the comma), but in the spirit of section 7.3. I take that property to be orthogonal to the question of internal structure. The embedded IP in (106) directly expresses the predication relation between the AP *rouge* and its subject NP *crayon*. *De* is the same D/P^0 as in (104). The difference in interpretation that holds between (104) and (106) is determined entirely within IP.

Quite similar (but without dislocation intonation) is the following, with fronting of a predicate NP:[53]

(107) cet   imbécile de Jean
      that imbecile of Jean

(108) cet [$_{D/PP}$[$_{NP}$ imbécile$_j$] [de [$_{IP}$ Jean I^0 [e]$_j$ ...

Although (105) has no counterpart in English, (107) may have one, if we abstract away from determiner differences (which, as Napoli (1989, p. 213) notes in her study of Italian and English, are independent of this construction).

(109) that idiot of a doctor

(110) that [$_{D/PP}$[$_{NP}$ idiot$_j$] [of [$_{IP}$ a doctor I^0 [e]$_j$ ...

The analysis indicated in (108)/(110) differs from Napoli's (1989, p. 206) in expressing in a direct and familiar way within IP the subject-predicate relation understood to hold between *Jean* and *imbécile* and between *a doctor* and *idiot*.

French has a third construction involving a predication interpretation and *de* that I will discuss in somewhat more detail.

(111) quelqu'un de célèbre
      someone   of famous

(112) Jean en   a   acheté trois de rouges.
      Jean of-them has bought three of red

(113) Jean a   acheté TROIS voitures de rouges (pas quatre).
      Jean has bought three   cars   of red   (not four)

(The best English renditions are *someone famous, Jean bought three red ones*, and *Jean bought THREE red cars (not four)*.) As discovered by Azoulay-Vicente (1985), this use of *de* before AP is found only in constructions that are plausibly analyzed as involving variables. The position of *quelqu'un* will be filled by a variable at LF, under standard assumptions. (113) involves focalization, which gives rise to an operator-variable structure in LF, following ideas going back to Chomsky 1976. The same sequence of words with no focal stress is ungrammatical.

(114) *Jean a acheté trois voitures de rouges.

Finally, Azoulay-Vicente (p. 228) argues that *en*-cliticization quite generally creates focalization on the quantifier/numeral left behind (*trois* in (112)).

It seems highly implausible to take these *de*-AP phrases to be complements of N (e.g., of *voitures* in (113)), if only because they seem so similar to relative clauses. (That similarity, in particular as concerns behavior with respect to the A-over-A Principle, in fact led to the suggestion in Kayne 1975, sec. 2.10, that *de*-AP phrases were of category S.) The plausibility of taking these phrases to be N complements is further diminished by the existence of some cases of "stacking."[54]

(115) quelqu'un d'autre de célèbre
       someone   of other of famous
       'someone else famous'

Let me take up, instead, the similarity between these *de*-AP phrases and relative clauses. As noted in the discussion following (8), relative clauses cannot be right-adjoined to any node. The same holds for *de*-AP, in all the examples just given. As in the case of relative clauses, I am consequently led to a raising/promotion analysis of *de*-AP phrases.

The required structure has in effect already been provided in (106), which parallels a standard relative clause structure, except that the IP is neither finite nor infinitival and the D/P⁰ *de* occurs instead of C⁰.[55] There are two possible ways of attributing to the *de*-AP construction the structure of (106). Starting from '[$_{D/PP}$[de [$_{IP}$ NP [I^0 AP]]]]', one could envisage moving NP to Spec,D/PP. With NP = *quelqu'un* and AP = *célèbre*, that would produce a string that looked like (111), but it would not provide any immediate means of accounting for the contrast between (113) and (114), or for certain other properties of this construction that I will address below. Finally, it would lead to a *that*-trace-type violation, with *de* playing the role of *that* (see the discussion of (57)).

The second possibility, which is not excluded by *that*-trace considerations, is to start from a structure like (106), except that the positions of
NP and AP are reversed.

(116) D^0 [$_{D/PP}$[de [$_{IP}$ AP [I^0 NP …

The NP then moves to Spec,D/PP, yielding (117).

(117) D^0 [$_{D/PP}$ NP$_j$ [de [$_{IP}$ AP [I^0 [$_{NP}$ e]$_j$ …

With NP = *quelqu'un* and AP = *célèbre*,[56] this again produces (111), as
desired.

In addition to a *that*-trace advantage, the proposal indicated in (117)
allows us to begin to understand the focalization requirement of (113)
versus (114), at the very least in terms of the fact that (105) itself involves
focalization of the AP *rouge* (and necessarily nonfocalization of the NP
crayon). In other words, there is a generalization in effect that spans those
D/PP structures headed by *de* that contain an IP complement of *de* that
expresses a predication relation.

As for why the otherwise comparable possessive structure of (104) does
not show the same effect, let me tentatively suggest that the difference
depends on the fact that the phrase in Spec,IP in (104) is a DP, whereas
the corresponding phrase in (106) is an NP and in (117) an AP. Now NP
and AP have in common that they are predicative categories and not
potential arguments, unlike DP. This makes it possible to state the distinction as follows: movement of NP/AP that crosses another predicative
category XP (where XP c-commands the starting position of NP/AP) and
also crosses a c-commanding *de* is possible only if the landing site is an
operator position;[57] that is, the trace left by such movement must be
interpreted as a variable.

We can now interpret (113) versus (114) as indicating that the NP (*trois
voitures*) moved to Spec,D/PP must receive focal stress in order to be
licensed as an operator binding that variable.[58] In addition, consider the
following contrast noted by Azoulay-Vicente (1985, p. 216):

(118) Qui de sérieux as-tu   rencontré?
       who of serious have-you met

(119) *Quel   homme d'intelligent connais-tu?
       what/which man   of intelligent know-you

Qui in (118) is the *wh*-counterpart of *quelqu'un*, so that *qui de sérieux* will
have the analysis given in (117). The deviance of (119) is unexpected, until

one notices the resemblance between this contrast and the one pointed out by Cinque (1990, p. 74) for Italian.

(120) Qualcosa, farò.
       something I-will-do

(121) Qualche sbaglio *(lo) fa   anche Gianni.
       some   mistake   it does also   Gianni

Preposing a non-*wh* DP in Italian is normally not possible in the absence of a coindexed clitic; (121) is a representative example. An exception is constituted by bare quantifiers such as *qualcosa*. Cinque takes such bare quantifier phrases to be intrinsic quantifiers, that is, to have the special property, as compared with *qualche sbaglio*, of being able to license a variable (in the position of the trace). The trace of a preposed DP must be licensed either as a variable or by a clitic, whence the observed contrast.

Now I have just suggested that the structure in (117) has the property that the trace of the moved NP must be a variable. This poses no problem in (118), on the reasonable assumption that French *qui* is also a bare quantifier.

(122) D^0 [$_{D/PP}$ qui$_j$ [de [$_{IP}$ sérieux [I^0 [$_{NP}$ e]$_j$ ...

On the other hand, *quel homme* in (119) is not a bare quantifier, just as *qualche sbaglio* is not, and therefore does not properly license its trace as a variable.[59] Note that the parallelism between the phenomenon studied by Cinque and the one under discussion here holds to a still greater level of detail, if it is correct to think that the focus-based contrast between (113) and (114) is essentially like the following one in Italian:

(123) GIANNI ho   visto.
       Gianni   I-have seen

(124) *Gianni ho visto.

Cinque notes that a preposed DP that is neither a bare quantifier nor a *wh*-phrase is legitimate if given focal stress, which licenses it as an operator-variable construction.[60]

Azoulay-Vicente (1985, p. 25) points out that *de*-AP does not allow a floating quantifier to the left of AP and that this contrasts with the behavior of ordinary relatives.

(125) Mireille en   a lu   dix qui sont tous intéressants.
       Mireille of-them has read 10 that are all   interesting

(126) *Mireille en   a   lu   dix de tous intéressants.
       Mireille of-them has read 10 of   all   interesting

Assuming Sportiche's (1988) reanalysis of floating quantifiers as stranded quantifiers, this follows from the fact that there is no pre-AP subject position in the *de*-construction in (117), although there is in the finite relative.[61]

The '[$_{IP}$ AP [I^0 NP ...]]' substructure of (116), which I have been arguing to be the optimal way of expressing the (partial) similarity between the *de*-AP construction and relative clauses, need not be taken to correspond to an initial structure. Without the main proposal being affected, it could well be that the AP is moved to Spec,IP from a post-NP position, so that a more accurate representation would be (127).

(127) [$_{IP}$ AP$_j$ [I^0 [NP [F^0 [e]$_j$]]]]

If so, this IP substructure would recall Moro's (1991; 1993) proposal concerning copula sentences like (128).

(128) The cause of the riot was a picture of the wall.

According to his proposal, the phrase *the cause of the riot* moves to Spec,IP from the predicate position within the small clause complement of the copula.[62]

(129) the cause$_i$ was [[a picture] [F^0 [e]$_i$]]

8.7 Nonrestrictive Relatives

In English nonrestrictive relatives contrast with restrictive relatives in that the former are associated with an intonation break, usually indicated by commas, that is absent in the latter.

(130) The young man, who I saw yesterday, is a linguist.

(131) The young man who I saw yesterday is a linguist.

I have argued that restrictive relatives must involve a structure of the form '[D^0 CP]', with movement of the relativized head (and *wh*-word) to Spec,CP. A priori, it might be that the intonation break present with nonrestrictives reflects a syntactic structure quite distinct from that of restrictives, for example, one in which the nonrestrictive is adjoined to NP or DP. However, right-adjunction is not compatible with the present theory.

I will prefer to pursue a different course and to reevaluate the significance of the intonation break in the light of the approach taken in section 7.3 concerning Romance right-dislocation. There I argued that the particular intonation associated with (Romance) right-dislocation is best understood as a PF property linked (probably via a feature present in the "overt" syntax) to an LF property of that construction, namely, that the right-dislocated phrase (or phrases) moves leftward in LF to a position in which a left-dislocated phrase (or phrases) could be found overtly. This means that the right-dislocated phrase actually occupies a complement position and that the special intonation in question is associated with that complement position.

The parallel proposal that I would like to make for relatives is that restrictives and nonrestrictives differ at LF but do not differ structurally in the overt syntax.[63] More specifically, nonrestrictives partake of the same '[D^0 CP]' structure as restrictives. Right-adjunction plays no role in nonrestrictives, any more than it does in restrictives.

The idea that UG treats the two types of relative clause in a more unified fashion than English might lead one to believe is supported by the claims made by Kuno (1973, p. 235), de Rijk (1972, p. 134), Keenan (1985, p. 169), Mosel and Hovdhaugen (1992, p. 635), and Craig (1977, p. 194), to the effect that Japanese, Basque, Malagasy, Samoan, and Jacaltec do not display the intonational (or other) differences between restrictives and nonrestrictives that English does.[64] On the other hand, English is not unique. French and Italian both have comparable intonational differences. As a first approximation, it appears that an obligatory intonational difference of the English sort is found only in languages with postnominal relatives. However, I do not think that the position of the noun (more exactly, the relativized NP) is at the heart of the intonational matter.

Consider, for example, the difference between the restrictive and nonrestrictive interpretation of English adjectives.

(132) John was telling us about the industrious Greeks.

Although it is slight, there seems to be a difference in intonation here, too. In section 8.4 I argued that prenominal adjectives can be derived from postnominal restrictive small clause relatives. A natural extension would be that on their nonrestrictive interpretation prenominal adjectives can be derived in parallel fashion and that the slight intonational difference between the two readings of (132) is akin to the more robust one seen in (130) versus (131). This suggests that it is not exactly the postnominal position of the full relative that is at issue with respect to the two types of relative, but the positional property that the English full relative shares with the English adjective, namely, the property of following the definite article.

It is not controversial to say that restrictives differ from nonrestrictives in that the former are in the scope of the definite article in (131) whereas the latter are not in the scope of the definite article in (130). It is natural to take this scope difference not to be a fact about overt syntactic structure but to be a fact about LF.

More specifically, the proposal is that both kinds of finite relative clause enter into the structure '[D^0 [$_{CP}$ NP [C^0 IP]]]', where NP has moved into Spec,CP from within IP. English restrictives and nonrestrictives share this property in the overt syntax. However, in nonrestrictives further movement takes place at LF; namely, IP moves to Spec,DP, yielding for nonrestrictives the structure (133).

(133) [$_{DP}$ IP$_i$ [D^0 [$_{CP}$ NP [C^0 [e]$_i$]]]]

Subsequent to this LF movement, the IP of the nonrestrictive is no longer within the scope of D^0.[65]

We can think of this LF movement as being triggered for nonrestrictives by a syntactic feature present in the overt syntax. We can then take the intonation break associated with English nonrestrictives to be determined in PF by the same feature. Assume that this feature is deleted immediately subsequent to IP-movement. In a language like English that deletion will take place in LF and will not be able to affect the presence of the feature in PF. Consequently, the feature will be present in PF to trigger the intonation break.[66]

Now consider a language that moves the IP of all relatives up to Spec,DP overtly. In such a language the relevant feature on nonrestrictives disappears before the point at which the derivation branches off to PF. Consequently, no intonation break is triggered. This accounts for the lack of intonation break for nonrestrictives in at least Japanese and Basque.[67]

The idea that nonrestrictives are essentially like restrictives in the overt syntax—and more specifically, that nonrestrictives, too, involve the raising/promotion of the relativized NP from within IP up to Spec,CP—is supported by the existence of reconstruction effects in nonrestrictives.

(134) These pictures of himself, which (Mary thinks that) John would be
        flattered to receive from us, are really quite awful.

If *pictures of himself* raises from the object position of *receive*, then the acceptability of (134) can be understood as in Chomsky 1993, pp. 37ff.[68] Similarly, there seems to me to be a slight Condition B effect in (135), akin to that in (136).

(135) These pictures of him, which John received yesterday, are of poor quality.

(136) John received these pictures of him yesterday.

And I find a partial Condition C effect in (137).

(137) Those stories about John, which he really gets upset at, are not even true.

Another kind of reason for thinking that nonrestrictives are in a strong sense syntactically parallel to restrictives concerns the kind of restriction found with French and Italian relative pronouns that was discussed starting at (13). The relative pronouns *qui* and *cui* can appear as prepositional objects with pied-piping of the preposition, but not as direct objects. This holds for nonrestrictives, too. For example, consider the French sentence (138).[69]

(138) *Jean, qui je connais bien, est intelligent.
        Jean who I know   well is intelligent

Under a raising/promotion approach to nonrestrictives, (138) can be accounted for as in the above discussion, in terms of the lack of an appropriate landing site for *Jean*. If nonrestrictives did not involve raising, it would be hard to see what to make of (138), in particular given that *qui* as direct object is in fact possible in free relatives (example from Hirschbühler and Rivero 1983, p. 517).[70]

(139) Qui tu as   rencontré est malade.
        who you have met   is sick

From the present perspective, (139) is not subject to the violation seen in (138) because it has no phrase corresponding to *Jean* at all, so that the landing site problem does not arise.

The analysis I have proposed for nonrestrictives implies that all non-PF differences between nonrestrictives and restrictives should be located at LF. For example, stacked relatives are possible (see (36)) if all are restrictive or if all are restrictive but the last.

(140) the book that's on the table, which I've read twice

If a nonrestrictive appears nonfinally, however, the result is bad.

(141) *the book, which I've read twice, that's on the table

(142) *the book, which I've read twice, which is on the table

In (140) *I've read twice* is the main IP of the CP sister to *the*. (*Which* is in Spec,CP and *book that's on the table* is in Spec,*which*.) In (141), on the other hand, *I've read twice* is an IP properly contained in *book, which I've read twice*, which is a phrase occupying Spec,CP. Thus, the desired distinction can be drawn if in '$[D^0 \, [_{CP} \, XP \, [C^0 \, IP]]]$' the IP sister to C^0 can move to the highest Spec,DP (when IP is nonrestrictive), but an IP embedded down within XP cannot. (This account of (141) carries over directly to (142).)

More precisely, (141) has the following form:

(143) $D^0[_{CP}[_{CP}$ book which $[C^0 \, IP]] \, [C^0 \, IP]]$

Movement of the rightmost IP to Spec,DP could be licensed by incorporation of the rightmost C^0 to D^0, as mentioned in the last paragraph of note 24. But movement of the leftmost IP to Spec,DP would have to involve movement of a right branch from within a left branch,[71] yielding a violation recalling that of the following example (see Kayne 1983b, n. 3; Chomsky 1986a, p. 31):

(144) *Who has the cold weather given the sister of a bad case of the flu?

Thus, the fact that a nonfinal relative in a sequence of stacked relatives must be restrictive is attributable to a combination of two factors: the movement constraint just discussed, plus the basic point that nonrestrictives undergo LF movement of IP, and restrictives do not.

Emonds (1979, p. 232) notes that there are no nonrestrictive counterparts to free relatives.

(145) John ate what(ever) they put in front of him.

If the variant without *ever* has some abstract counterpart to *ever*, then it might be possible to relate the absence of free nonrestrictives to a parallel contrast involving *every*.

(146) John ate every cookie they baked.

(147) *John ate every cookie, which they baked.

Apparently, the variable in object position bound by *every* in (146) must remain within the scope of *every* at LF and is not allowed to be moved out of its scope by IP-movement to Spec, *every*.[72]

A further difference between restrictives and nonrestrictives concerns idiom chunks, which occur only in the former, as noted by Vergnaud (1974, p. 181).

(148)   the headway that we made

(149)   *the headway, which we made

This is compatible with assigning the same overt syntactic structure to the two kinds of relative. In (149) (but not in (148)) the trace of the idiom chunk is moved along with the rest of IP to Spec,DP at LF. Thus, the resulting deviance can arguably be related to that of (151).

(150)   Advantage is likely to be taken of us.

(151)   *How likely to be taken of us is advantage?

In both (149) (in LF) and (151) the c-command relation between the idiom chunk and its trace is destroyed.[73]

Chapter 9

Extraposition

9.1 Relative Clause Extraposition

Sentences like (1) and (2) have frequently been analyzed in terms of rightward movement ("extraposition") of the relative clause.[1]

(1) Something just happened that you should know about.

(2) Someone just walked into the room who we don't know.

The usual assumption is then that the extraposed relative is right-adjoined to some phrasal node, say, VP or IP. Which node it might be is not important here, since right-adjunction is excluded by the present LCA-based theory independently of the category label of the node adjoined to.

Attachment of the extraposed relative under VP (e.g., as a sister to both *walked* and *into the room* in (2)) is likewise impossible, since that would create a ternary-branching structure that would violate the LCA as a result of *into the room* and the relative clause c-commanding each other (which would lead to a violation of antisymmetry). A third possibility that might come to mind especially for (1) would be that the relative moves down into the complement position directly to the right of V. However, this does not seem very plausible (in particular if *happen* is an unaccusative verb, with a trace of *something* as complement). In addition, the last two possibilities mentioned suffer from a problem concerning the trace of the extraposed relative, which would not be c-commanded by its antecedent. This trace-binding problem would not arise if the relative were right-adjoined to IP, but since right-adjunction is sharply prohibited by the present theory, I conclude that none of the three possibilities is viable and that a rightward movement analysis of relative clause "extraposition" is not correct.

The problem with rightward movement here is in essence a landing site problem and therefore cannot be solved by base-generating the relative clause in one of the landing site positions just considered. Just like right-adjunction in the case of movement, base generation of the relative in a position right-adjoined to VP or IP is prohibited by the fact that asymmetric c-command must map to precedence.[2] Base generation of the relative as sister to both *walked* and *into the room* is also prohibited, exactly as in the previous paragraph. Base generation of the relative as the direct complement of V is implausible. For example, if *happen* is unaccusative in (1), the complement must be *something*, and if *happen* is not unaccusative, it should have no complement.

From an acquisition standpoint, the fact that the present theory rules out several logically possible analyses for this construction is a highly desirable result, since it means that the learner in this case is free of the burden of having to choose from among too many competing analyses. It is, of course, essential that the theory make available at least one analysis. What is available, but not yet discussed, is the possibility of instead taking the "extraposed" relative to be "stranded" by leftward movement of *something/someone*.[3]

(3) Something$_i$ just happened [[e]$_i$ that you ...

(4) Someone$_i$ just walked into the room [[e]$_i$ who ...

This reanalysis of relative clause extraposition as relative clause stranding, which recalls Sportiche's (1988) reanalysis of quantifier floating as quantifier stranding,[4] straightforwardly eliminates the trace-binding problem. There is now no relative clause trace at all that needs to be bound.

The trace of *something/someone* is bound by the phrase in subject position in the familiar way. (It should be noted that, as in Sportiche's proposal, this analysis assumes crucially that subjects can move up into Spec,IP from a lower position.)

Compared with relative clause extraposition, relative clause stranding has the further advantage that it provides a better account of the existence in this construction of a restriction known as the Right Roof Constraint (Ross 1967).[5] Consider the following example:

(5) *The fact that somebody walked into the room is irrelevant who I knew.

In extraposition terms, the relative *who I knew* is seen to be unable to move out of its minimal clause, though why it could not do so in successive-cyclic fashion was never clear, as Larson and May (1990, p. 112n.) note.

If instead what is involved is leftward movement of *somebody*, then there is an immediate double violation in (5). First, *somebody* would have to originate within *somebody who I knew*, and therefore the entire phrase *somebody who I knew* would have to be in the complement position of the matrix predicate.

(6) the fact that [e] walked into the room is irrelevant somebody who I knew

But since *irrelevant* takes no direct complement (i.e., that position is not a theta-position), the phrase *somebody who I knew* would not be assigned a theta-role. Second, the movement of *somebody* into the empty embedded subject position in (6) would constitute movement to a noncommanding position.[6]

Compared with relative clause extraposition, relative clause stranding has another advantage as well: it provides a more direct account of the fact that the relative clause, when separated from its 'head,' appears to the right of that head, rather than to its left.

(7) *That you should know about, something just happened.

(8) *Who we don't know, someone just walked into the room.

If relative clauses could be moved rightward out of DP, why not also leftward?

The stranding proposal provides the following account of (7)/(8). First, one could not derive them by starting from a structure like *Something that you should know about just happened*, where *something that you should know about* was (somehow) in topic position, and then moving *someone/ something* down into subject position, since that would leave an unbound trace. Nor could (7), for example, be derived from *Something that you should know about just happened* by leftward movement of *that you should know about*, since that constituent, under the analysis of relatives proposed above, is not a full CP. Instead, it corresponds only to the lower segment of a two-segment CP (in standard X-bar terms, to a single-bar category).

(9) [$_{CP}$ something$_i$ [$_{CP}$ that you should know about [e]$_i$]]

Given the discussion in the last two paragraphs of section 3.1 (also see (the text to) note 25 of chapter 8), we know that the lower segment of a two-segment category cannot be moved at all.[7]

Finally, (7) cannot be derived from a structure like (3) by moving the entire CP (including the trace of *something*) leftward, which would yield (10).

(10) *[[e]$_i$ that you ...]$_j$ something$_i$ just happened [e]$_j$

The reason is that the initial trace '[e]$_i$' is not properly bound.[8]

This kind of violation may underlie the well-known fact that VP-preposing cannot carry along an "extraposed" relative while leaving the "head" behind in subject position.[9]

(11) *John said that something would happen to him that you should know about, and happen to him that you should know about, something did.

(12) ... and happen to him [[e]$_i$ that ...], something$_i$ did

Again, the trace of the raising of *something* to Spec,IP has been carried along by VP-preposing in such a way that it is no longer c-commanded by its antecedent.

The contrasting fact that VP-preposing can carry along an "extraposed" object relative is immediately understandable (example essentially from Baltin 1987, p. 588).

(13) John said that he would call people up who are from Boston, and call people up who are from Boston he will.

In (13) VP-preposing has taken along both the relative and its raised "head," so that the trace-binding violation of (11) does not hold.

(14) ... and [call people$_i$ up [[e]$_i$ who ...]] he will

As seen in (14), the c-command relation between *people* and its trace is unaffected by the preposing of the VP.[10]

From the perspective of Chomsky 1993 and the work leading up to it, relative clause extraposition has the disadvantage of being purely optional.

(15) Someone just walked into the room who we don't know.

(16) Someone who we don't know just walked into the room.

It is hard to see what kind of trigger could plausibly be at issue. A stranding approach leads to a different characterization. As seen in (4), the phrase *someone who we don't know* in (15) is sentence-final at the point at which *someone* moves to subject position. (16) can be taken to share that structure, except that in (16) it is the entire phrase *someone who we don't know* that moves. Both movements could plausibly be attributed to a need for Case.

The stranded relative clause cannot be found between the verb and its complement.

(17) *Someone just walked who we don't know into the room.

From a stranding point of view, this suggests that *someone who we don't know* could not appear there, prior to leftward movement of *someone*. There may thus be a relation between (17) and (18)/(19)

(18) There just walked into the room someone who we don't know.

(19) *There just walked someone who we don't know into the room.

(vs. *John ushered someone who we don't know into the room*).

The order of phrases that holds in (18) is reminiscent of the order in (20).

(20) John ushered into the room someone who we don't know.

I argued in section 7.2 that sentences like (20) involve leftward movement and raising of the PP across the direct object. Correspondingly, I will propose that in (18) the PP *into the room* has raised across *someone who we don't know*. In the resulting structure *into the room* asymmetrically c-commands *someone who we don't know*. In the discussion above example (21) of chapter 7, I suggested that the direct object in (20) might be in a non-Case position below the normal position for English direct objects. If *someone who we don't know* in (18) is in that same position, and if it cannot be there in (19), then it is possible to formulate the following restriction (in effect a subcase of the prohibition against movement from one structural case position to another; see Chomsky 1993, p. 32):

(21) A relative clause can be stranded by A-movement only in a
       non-Case position.

If *into the room* asymmetrically c-commands *someone who we don't know* in (18), and if (15) is derived from a structure resembling (18), then it is clear that in (15) the stranded relative is asymmetrically c-commanded by the PP (as we would expect from general considerations, given the LCA and the prohibition against right-adjunction). This is supported by facts concerning the licensing of *any*. Consider the following sentence, under the wide scope reading of the negation:

(22) ?A man walked into no room.

This sentence under that interpretation is not very natural, but allowing for that, the contrast between (23) and (24)/(25) is notable (see Larson 1988).[11]

(23) *A man who had any money walked into no room.

(24) ??A man walked into no room who had any money.

(25) ??A man walked into no room who anybody knew.

The negation within the PP cannot license an instance of *any* within the subject phrase, as expected. To some extent, however, it can license an instance of *any* within the stranded relative, supporting the idea that in (24)/(25) the relative is lower than the PP.[12]

Somewhat similar is the pair of examples noted by Guéron (1980, p. 650).

(26) A picture of Mary was sent to her.

(27) A picture was sent to her of Mary.

(26) involves PP-extraposition, which I must reanalyze as PP-stranding in a way parallel to relative clause stranding.[13] Again, *of Mary* in (27) must be lower than *to her* (given the unavailability of right-adjunction). The fact that it is lower allows one to understand, in terms of Condition C and c-command (abstracting away from *to*), why *her* can refer to *Mary* in (26), but not in (27).

On the other hand, Reinhart (1983, pp. 49, 127) gives examples of relative clause stranding (in my terms) that appear parallel to (27) but are nonetheless natural with coreference.

(28) Nobody would ever call her before noon who knows anything
      about Rosa's weird sleeping habits.

Here, *her* and *Rosa* can be coreferential. The problem is that the same reasoning (unavailability of right-adjunction) that has led me to conclude that in (27) *of Mary* must be lower than (i.e., asymmetrically c-commanded by) *to her* leads directly to the conclusion that in (28) the stranded relative *who knows anything about Rosa's* ... must be lower than *her*, in which case we would apparently expect a Condition C violation.

I think the solution is to recall, first, that Condition C applies under reconstruction (see Chomsky 1993, pp. 40ff.), and second, that in the analysis of (18) proposed above the 'V PP DP' order is derived by leftward movement of PP past the subject DP. Keeping in mind that the stranded relative in (28) is part of the subject DP, this analysis of (18) transposed to (28) yields the following conclusion: in (28) *her* (and also *before noon*) reaches its visible position as a result of leftward movement across the subject DP, which includes the stranded relative.

The reconstruction that Chomsky (1993) discusses with respect to Condition C is of the *wh*-movement variety. Assume that scrambling of the sort that moves *her* across the subject DP in (28) interacts in the same way as *wh*-movement with Condition C. Then, in the case of (28), condition C will look at an LF representation in which *her* is in fact below the stranded relative—in which case, *her* does not (at that level of representation) c-command *Rosa*, so that there is no Condition C violation, as desired.

Reconstruction of scrambling in (28) yields subject-object order. Putting this another way, and abstracting away from the position of the verb, reconstruction in (28) yields subject-predicate order. Now, so-called presentational sentences (see Guéron 1980) arguably do not "want" to have a simple subject-predicate representation at LF. Assume that this translates into the conclusion that reconstruction of scrambling does not hold for presentational sentences. Then the potential Condition C violation found in (28) would not be undone at LF in a presentational sentence of the same general form as (28) itself. To my ear, this expectation is borne out.

(29) All of a sudden, a man appeared to Mary who had once been in love with her.

(30) All of a sudden, a man appeared to her who had once been in love with Mary.

Coreference between *Mary* and *her* seems natural in (29) but very difficult to accept in (30), as expected if *to her* in (30) does not reconstruct (because of the presentational character of (30)) and if *to her* there asymmetrically c-commands the stranded relative.

Note that none of the above implies that a stranded relative clause is necessarily an island, in particular since the position of the object in (20) is not (example repeated from (18) of chapter 7).

(31) the problem which I explained to John only part of

And in fact stranded relative clauses are definitely not islands in Norwegian (see Taraldsen 1981, sect. 2) and to some extent are not even in English, as Chung and McCloskey (1983, p. 708) have shown.[14]

(32) That's one trick that I've known a lot of people who've been taken
        in by.

(In essence following Taraldsen, I take (32) to involve relative clause stranding, even though in this example the effect of raising *a lot of people* happens not to be visible.)

Ziv and Cole (1974) have observed that relative clause extraposition (now stranding) is difficult with *the*.

(33)   A man just walked in who we knew in high school.

(34)   ??The man just walked in who we knew in high school.

I would like to interpret this contrast as reflecting the mixture of two different judgments that hold with *the*, which can be made clearer if the appropriate word is added to (34).

(35)   The very man just walked in that I had been telling her about.

(36)   *The only man just walked in that I had mentioned to her.

(The ungrammaticality of (36) was pointed out by Guéron (1980, p. 650).) The idea is that English *the* is ambiguous (in a way to be clarified below) between the *the* of (35) and that of (36), and that this is what is behind the uncertain judgment concerning (34).

Let me begin with the sharp contrast between (33) and (36). In (33) *a man* is moved leftward from within the DP *a man who we knew in high school*. That DP has the structure 'D CP', and similarly for *the only man that I had mentioned to her* in (36). In chapter 8, I quite generally took *the* to correspond to D, and *man* to have been moved to Spec,CP. If so, then, independently of the exact position of *only*, it is clear that *the only man* in *the only man that I had mentioned to her* cannot be a constituent. Under standard assumptions, it therefore cannot be moved. This accounts for the ungrammaticality of (36).

In part along the lines of Perlmutter (1970), there is no reason to take English *a* to be of the same category as *the*. More precisely, I take *a* in (33) not to correspond to the D of 'D CP', but rather to be included in Spec,CP along with *man*. Consequently, *a man* can be moved leftward as a constituent into Spec,IP (probably passing through Spec,DP), yielding (33).[15]

To allow (35), I will adopt a suggestion made by Jae Hong Lee (personal communication), to the effect that *the* there is really a demonstrative, whereas it cannot plausibly be taken to be a demonstrative in (36). In particular, although *the* in (35) can be replaced fairly naturally by *that*, such replacement in (36) is completely impossible.

Consider more specifically Szabolsci's (to appear) discussion of Hungarian, and the fact she points out about demonstratives and the definite article in Hungarian, namely, that demonstratives can follow the definite article (and be separated from it by a possessor phrase). From an LCA perspective, this means that Hungarian demonstratives can occur lower than the definite article. I will jump from that to the proposal that English demonstrative *the* can occur with *man* (and with *very*) in Spec,CP: 'D [$_{CP}$ the very man [that [$_{IP}$ ...]]]', where *the very man* binds a trace within IP. Given this structure, *the very man* can move out of DP (again, probably through Spec,DP), ending up in Spec,IP in (35). If this *the* can to some extent occur without *very* (or *same*), then (34) will be acceptable to that extent (and similarly for Norwegian; see Taraldsen 1981, pp. 488–489).

As mentioned in the last paragraph of note 20 of chapter 8, a stranded relative can sometimes occur without either a *wh*-word or *that*.

(37) ?A book just came out I've been meaning to read.

This contrasts sharply with (38).

(38) *Whatever books came out late I wanted to read.

Setting aside the irrelevant reading where *whatever books came out late* is a topicalized object, (38) cannot possibly be an instance of relative clause stranding, with *whatever books* the head of *I wanted to read* (cf. *Whatever books I wanted to read came out late*).

This very general fact was noted by Bresnan and Grimshaw (1978, p. 346n.), who phrased it in terms of relative clause extraposition. From the present perspective, the generalization is that free relatives never give rise to relative clause stranding. The question is why (38) is not derivable from a structure like '[e] came out late whatever books I wanted to read'. Recalling note 13 of chapter 8, the answer is that *whatever books* is not a constituent. Rather, *ever* is a D outside CP to which the *wh*-word incorporates. Thus, (38) is impossible for essentially the same reason as (36).[16]

The (standard) assumption that movement applies only to constituents, which I have used to account for (36) and (38), appears to pose a problem as far as (39) is concerned.

(39) John is going to talk to someone tomorrow who he has a lot of faith in.

If this kind of example is taken to be parallel to those previously discussed,[17] then it should be derived from a structure resembling '... to talk tomorrow to someone who ...' (where *tomorrow* probably has previously moved leftward across the whole PP) via leftward movement of *to someone*, stranding the relative. The problem is that in *to someone who ...*, *to someone* is not obviously a constituent.[18]

Consider the following approach, which would allow *to someone* to in fact be a constituent. Start from the standard PP structure 'P DP', with *someone* inside Spec,CP: 'to [$_{DP}$ D [$_{CP}$ someone ...]]'. Let *someone* move to Spec,PP (probably via Spec,DP), yielding 'someone$_i$ [to [$_{DP}$ D [$_{CP}$ [e]$_i$ ...'.[19] Then let *to* left-adjoin to *someone*: '[$_{QP}$ to [$_{QP}$ someone]]'.[20] Subsequent leftward movement of this newly created QP out of Spec,PP will allow (39).

9.2 Result Clauses and Comparatives

Result clauses occur in a construction that to some extent resembles relative clause stranding.

(40) So many people came to the party that there wasn't enough to eat.

An important difference between the two constructions has been discussed by Guéron and May (1984).

(41) Plots by so many conspirators have been hatched that the government is helpless.

(42) *Plots by many conspirators have been hatched who work for the government.

From the perspective of the preceding section, (42) is ungrammatical because starting from a structure like '[e] have been hatched plots by many conspirators who ...', there is no way to reach (42) by leftward movement of *plots by many conspirators*, stranding *who ...*, since *plots by many conspirators* is not a constituent.

The fact that (41) is grammatical suggests, then, that result clauses are not (necessarily) instances of stranding. On the other hand, they cannot be taken to be right-adjoined to VP, IP, or CP, either. Let me propose, therefore, that the structure of (41) is (43).

(43) [[plots by so many ... hatched] [that [the ...]]]

The sentence as a whole is headed by the *that* that introduces the result clause. The part of the sentence preceding *that* is a clause occupying Spec,*that*.

The structure indicated in (43) correctly allows for the possibility that a pronoun in the left-hand clause will be coreferential with a lexical DP in the result clause.

(44) She has so much money now that Mary is the envy of all her classmates.

With *she has so much money now* in Spec,*that*, *she* does not c-command *Mary*.

Contrasting with (41) is (45).

(45) *Plots that so many people know about have been hatched that the government has lost all credibility.

I follow Rouveret (1978) and Guéron and May (1984) in taking this to indicate that *so* is required to raise at LF for the construction to be licensed. Given (43), the raising should presumably be to a position c-commanding *that*, yielding a kind of spec-head agreement configuration. Such LF raising is possible in (41), but it is not possible in (45) because *so* in (45) is too deeply embedded.[21]

(44) contrasts with (47).[22]

(46) John has so much money that he doesn't know what to do with it.

(47) He has so much money that John doesn't know what to do with it.

Coreference between *he* and *John* does not seem possible in (47). It may be that (47) has the structure (48),

(48) he has [so much money [that [John ...]]]

where *so much money* is in Spec,*that*—in effect, a kind of ECM structure. (Note that (43) itself can be thought of as akin to an ECM structure, perhaps with an abstract higher head (see section 4.3) in the specifier of the complement of which we find what is generally taken to be the main clause.)

Chomsky (1981, pp. 81–83) observes that comparatives display double behavior.

(49) Pictures of more people are for sale than I expected.

(50) *Pictures of more people are for sale than I met yesterday.

His discussion of (50) is in terms of extraposition. From the present perspective, the fact that (50) is parallel to (42) suggests that some comparative sentences should be analyzed as instances of stranding. Thus, (51) will be given the analysis in (52).

(51) More people are here today than I met yesterday.

(52) [e] are here today [more people than I met yesterday]

In (52) *more people* raises to Spec,IP, stranding the comparative clause *than I met yesterday* and yielding (51).

What about the internal structure of *more people than* ...? The *than*-clause cannot plausibly be a complement of *people*, nor can it be right-adjoined. Let me propose, rather, a structure parallel to that of (48).

(53) [more people [than [...]]]

The head of the entire phrase is *than*. *More people* is in Spec,*than*.

The natural next step is to attribute to (49) a structure parallel to that of (43).

(54) [pictures of more people ... sale [than [I expected ...

Than is again the head of the whole, but here its specifier contains a clause. LF movement of *more* will come into play, as with *so* in result constructions.

The fact that (50) is ill formed implies that it cannot have the structure shown in (54). Perhaps *than* can have a clausal specifier only if the gap in the complement clause of *than* is itself clausal.[23]

PART IV

Chapter 10
Conclusion

Starting from the intuition that a parsimonious UG would not have linear order and hierarchical structure be as independent of one another as syntactic theory normally assumes, I have proposed a Linear Correspondence Axiom (LCA) that brings hierarchical structure and linear order together. It does so by establishing a mapping between asymmetric c-command and linear precedence[1] and requiring that the result of the mapping be a full linear ordering of the terminals of the phrase marker in question.

From this perspective, linear order turns out to be more fundamental to syntax than is normally thought.[2] As a result of the LCA, the property of antisymmetry that a linear ordering has is inherited by the hierarchical structure. I have argued that this is behind X-bar theory, or rather, that X-bar theory, although largely accurate in its standard form, should not be considered to be a primitive part of syntactic theory (i.e., of UG).[3] What is primitive in UG is the LCA, from which follow familiar X-bar-theoretic properties such as (1) the need for a phrase to have a head, (2) the impossibility for a phrase to have more than one head, (3) the limitation to one specifier per phrase, (4) the limitation to one sister complement per head, and (5) the requirement that a complement not be a bare head.

Combined with a fairly standard definition of c-command in terms of category (as opposed to segment), the LCA goes beyond X-bar theory in the extent to which it limits phrase structure diversity. The LCA limits adjunctions to one per phrase or head adjoined to. In the case of adjunctions to phrases, that amounts to saying that there is no distinction between adjunctions and specifiers.

Extending the LCA-based theory to subword structure derives Williams's (1981) right-hand head generalization for morphology and leads to the proposal that clitics must adjoin to empty heads rather than to (finite) verbs.

I have derived the result that specifier-head-complement order is the only order made available by UG and consequently that there can be no directionality parameter for word order.

The empirical ramifications of these proposals are vast, and I have attempted to explore only a small fraction of them, hoping to give a sense of the kinds of advantages they offer. Time will tell whether the advantages are as one-sided as I presently think.

It is difficult to show with any degree of certainty that a particular theory of syntax is systematically more restrictive than others. Yet I think it plausible to claim that the present theory does not force one to introduce mechanisms that are not already (implicitly) part of syntactic theory. Although the prohibition against multiple adjunctions leads me to posit numerous abstract functional heads, I do not think that other theories can do without such entities.

If it is true that no (or few) new mechanisms are needed under this LCA-based theory, then we can focus without hesitation on the ways in which it has achieved substantially increased restrictiveness: no rightward adjunction movement rules are permitted, no right-adjunctions are permitted in the base; there is never a choice available between multiple left-adjunctions and multiple heads each with one specifier; no right-hand specifier positions are available; no left-hand complement positions are available; and all the advantages in restrictiveness of binary branching are maintained.[4]

To a significant extent, the LCA-based theory of syntax proposed here allows us to have the all too infrequent pleasure of seeing the theory choose the analysis.

Notes

Chapter 1

1. Strictly speaking, the term should be *left-locally total*.

2. See Kayne 1984, chaps. 6 and 7.

Chapter 2

1. Note that $\langle j, p \rangle$ corresponds to both $d\langle J, N \rangle$ and $d\langle J, P \rangle$.

2. These two cases differ only in that in one instance M and P stand for identically labeled nodes and in the other they do not. Whether M and P are identical in category or not has no effect on the way in which the LCA applies here.

3. The question arises of what happens if *John* (or any phrase) is moved. If the result of movement is that DP (or NP) dominates just a trace, then *see* and that trace will not be ordered at all with respect to one another, since the internal structure of DP (or NP), which ensured antisymmetry, will have been lost. This might conceivably be a tolerable consequence, since traces are in any event not visible. It is notable, though, that this question does not arise if movement transformations leave a copy rather than a trace (see Chomsky 1993).

4. Where antisymmetry is in addition violated by $\langle q, t \rangle$ and $\langle t, q \rangle$.

5. See Larson 1990, p. 595, Munn 1992, and Thiersch 1993.

Chapter 3

1. In the sense of Chomsky (1986a, p. 9): X excludes Y if no segment of X dominates Y.

2. The category P consisting of the two segments does not c-command Q by virtue of the exclusion part of the definition of c-command.

3. $\langle R, M \rangle$ is not in this set because P, which dominates R, does not dominate M, since only one of its segments dominates M.

   $\langle M, R \rangle$ is in A here since every category dominating M dominates R. This holds vacuously if P is the root node, nonvacuously otherwise. (The vacuous case could be eliminated by specifying in the definition of c-command "... and every category *or segment* that dominates X dominates Y"; but that would prevent c-command from out of adjunction configurations, in the sense discussed below.)

4. Without the segment/category distinction, and hence without specifiers or adjoined phrases, UG would be significantly less rich than we know it to be. On the other hand, it is worth noting that certain phrases, such as PP, DP, and NP, typically display no specifier (or adjoined phrase) and that if Agr$_{(S)}$ could bear a theta-role while still being a pure head of AgrP, then a verb could have a subject without having a specifier. If one were speculating about the evolution of UG, one would therefore be led to consider the possibility of a stage lacking the category/segment distinction.

5. See Fukui 1986 on Japanese. From the present perspective, there is a basic distinction between heads (categories that dominate no nonterminal) and nonheads (categories that dominate at least one nonterminal). Within the class of nonheads, a further distinction can be made between those that have a phrase adjoined to them and those that do not. See also the second paragraph of note 7.

6. See Kayne 1991, p. 649. The text proposal does not by itself prohibit the adjoined clitic from moving farther up; see Roberts 1991 and Kayne 1991, p. 661n.

7. See Chomsky 1986a, p. 4. The text prediction is incompatible with the movement of *to*-VP proposed in Kayne 1985, p. 115 (for recent discussion of particle constructions, see den Dikken 1992) and is similarly incompatible with Van Riemsdijk's (1989) analysis of *Bücher habe ich keine mehr* 'books have I no more' as involving movement of X^1. Den Besten and Webelhuth's (1990) analysis of German remnant topicalization is compatible with the text prediction as long as the XP moved out of the to-be-topicalized VP is not adjoined to that VP (rather, the XP must move higher).

Chomsky's (1986a, p. 6) proposal that adjunction to an argument is prohibited (see McCloskey 1992) could perhaps be derived if arguments all had to move (by LF) and if what a specifier is adjoined to is not an argument.

8. Note that the category M does not dominate Q, so that there is no need to take M to dominate itself. On the contrary, it is in all probability preferable that dominance be irreflexive. See Chomsky 1986a, n. 11. Compare also the irreflexivity of asymmetric c-command and of linear precedence itself, which I argued earlier to be significantly similar to dominance.

9. Note that the category M does not dominate q, since only one of its segments does.

10. See Chomsky and Lasnik 1993, sec. 3; also the observations in Kayne 1975, secs. 2.3, 2.4, to the effect that clitics in French are never phrasal.

Note that if the head to which the nonhead was adjoined had no complement structure at all, then the violation displayed in the text would not occur; however, with no complement structure, there would be no source for the adjoined phrase. On compounds, see below in section 4.5.

11. Recall that K asymmetrically c-commands Q since every category dominating K dominates Q (so that K c-commands Q), whereas Q does not exclude K (so that Q cannot c-command K).

12. This constituent structure may turn out to be supported by the fact that Italian dative clitic doubling is facilitated by the presence of an adjacent accusative clitic; see Cinque 1990, p. 178, n. 4.

13. These are the [+person] clitics, in the terms used in Kayne 1993, sec. 3.6.

14. This formulation would prohibit analyzing (i) as involving adjunction of *ne* to *vous.*

(i) Jean ne   vous voit jamais.
    Jean NEG you sees never
    'Jean never sees you.'

Ne must then either be sitting in an independent functional head position Neg^0, as proposed in Kayne 1989b, or have been cliticized as in Pollock 1989 to a head distinct from *vous.*

The order *vous ne*, with *vous* an object clitic (and similarly for *me, te, nous, se*), is found in some Romance languages/dialects (see Butz 1981; Parry 1984). It probably involves the adjunction of that object clitic to *ne.*

15. See the discussion in Kayne 1975, sec. 2.16; also Postal 1990.

16. Similarly, the construction given in (i), from Rooryck 1992, should probably be analyzed as having the first clitic, *lui*, adjoined to Agr = /z/, and the second, *en*, adjoined to the next functional head below that Agr.

(i) Donne lui-   /z/ -en
    give him/her$_{DAT}$ of-it
    'Give him/her (some) of it.'

17. Compare Rizzi's (1991) reinterpretation of May's (1985, p. 17) *Wh*-Criterion.

According to Webelhuth (1992, p. 129), relative clauses like the one in *John Smith, pictures of whom I have never liked, is . . .* are limited to English, among the Germanic languages. This could be accounted for if the other Germanic languages had a condition on relative *wh*-elements parallel to (24). Italian relative *il quale* acts like (literary) English, but Italian relative *cui* does not (see Cinque 1978); in *il cui libro* 'the who$_{GEN}$ book', *il cui* must probably count as a *wh*-element, unless *il* is adjoined to *cui.*

The question of what precisely makes *what city, which book* into *wh*-phrases in the text sense is left open. Hungarian *Mari melyik kalapja* 'Mary$_i$ which hat-Agr$_i$', from Szabolcsi, to appear, indicates that the *wh*-word does not universally need to overtly be in the highest specifier position of the *wh*-phrase.

18. The text proposal could be recast in Chomsky's (1993, p. 32) terms, given that my proposal about specifiers would mean that the specifier of the specifier of a head is in the checking domain of that head.

Note that (23) seems to show that LF movement of the sort that May (1985, p. 69) appeals to in order to account for the (for me some what marginal) bound variable reading of *Somebody from every city despises it* is too powerful, in that it would permit (23) to be saved.

The absence of pied-piping with *whose* + gerund discussed by Webelhuth (1992, p. 133) could, from my perspective, suggest that gerunds have an extra layer of structure (like CP) as compared with (derived) nominals and that *who(se)* in gerunds is necessarily always below that level.

19. See Taraldsen 1978 on Scandinavian.
   (22) and (23) are ungrammatical in all registers of English.

20. More specifically, Van Riemsdijk's proposal is that *what* moves through a Comp position associated with PP. In present terms, his proposal would imply that there is at least one functional head associated with and above P^0; see also Koopman 1993b. For my purposes, what is most important is that in (26) *what* move in LF into the specifier position of the highest such functional head. See the discussion of (33) in the text.

21. I have found one speaker of English who allows movement to Spec,PP to be followed at least sometimes by movement to Spec,CP of the whole PP, yielding sentences like %*What about are you thinking?*

22. Partially as in Huang and Tang 1991, p. 266, on Chinese *ziji*. Note that my claim that specifiers are adjoined and hence c-command out of the containing phrase might allow dispensing with Huang and Tang's notion "sub-command." The notion "closer c-commander" would recall proposals made by Rizzi (1990b) and Chomsky (1973, p. 270; 1993), and "potential antecedent" Chomsky's (1973, p. 262) notion "possible controller."

23. For important discussion of a language where Condition C appears not to hold, see Jayaseelan 1991.

24. See Aoun and Sportiche 1981 for data from (certain speakers of) Lebanese Arabic. Clitic doubling in Arabic might be amenable to an analysis along the lines of section 7.3.

25. This account requires the (reasonable) assumption that neither C^0 nor any other functional head is automatically available in root sentences in a position above IP, so that in these languages *gestern* is not adjoinable to any higher projection, either.

26. Apart from interrogatives. Notice that interrogatives with inversion are part of all registers of English, whereas (41) is not colloquial.

27. For reasons that are unclear (as in the contrast with German). Note that the parallelism between (43) and (44) is also found in C-less relatives, as noted by Doherty (to appear). Parallel facts are found in Swedish (for which Platzack (1985, p. 45) suggests a different interpretation).

28. Alongside the prohibition against two specifier positions, there is a prohibition that follows from the LCA against a head having two sister complements, since '[X YP ZP]' will yield a violation of antisymmetry (YP and ZP will c-command each other). A head can have more than one "complement" only by grouping them into small clauses, as in Kayne 1981c and especially Larson 1988, with the essential addition of a head position internal to each small clause.

29. In the theory assumed by Sportiche and the other references mentioned just above, phrasal movements can be either to specifier positions or to adjoined positions. In the present theory, the choice between licensing a phrase via a spec-head configuration and licensing it via an adjunction relation is not a real one.

All cases of apparent multiple adjunction to the same nonhead must involve either covert heads, as in the discussion of (39), or else absorption, as in Chomsky 1993, where one (*wh-*)phrase adjoins to another (possible in the present framework only if the one adjoined to has no other specifier).

The structures proposed by May (1985, p. 34) for multiple QR and the formulation of his Scope Principle are not compatible with the text proposals.

30. I use the term much as in Muysken 1982; that is, it refers either to '[ZP [X YP]]' or to an '[X YP]' to which nothing is adjoined (i.e., that has no specifier).

The root phrase itself will be unlicensed in the text sense unless it is sister to an abstract head, a possibility that I will return to later.

31. In addition to being affected by the intrinsic properties of specifier and head, the matching question will be affected by locality conditions, in particular by Relativized Minimality (Rizzi 1990b)/Economy ("shortest movement"; Chomsky 1993).

Adnominal adjective phrases that are not complements must then be specifiers, each of a separate head, a position that has been argued for on independent grounds by Cinque (1992; 1993b); see also section 8.4.

The same must hold for adverb phrases.

32. Left open is the question of what determines when Agr^0 has phonetic realization, and what features of the specifier can or must be reflected in that realization.

33. This exclusion of (47) is essentially akin to the exclusion of (3) of chapter 2.

34. The proposal in Kayne 1991, p. 668, to the effect that French *de* can be in Spec,CP can now be correct only if interpreted to mean that '[$_{PP}$[$_P$ de]]' can be in Spec,CP.

Chapter 4

1. See Bach 1971, p. 160. Ultan (1978, p. 229) mentions one language (Khasi) that appears to have question words in sentence-final position. In languages like Hungarian, the interrogative phrase, although not sentence-initial, clearly seems to precede the head it is associated with.

2. This point is made by Johnson (1991, p. 584).

3. See Emonds 1980 and many more recent works.

4. See the convincing arguments given by Ordóñez (1994) in favor of the idea that in Spanish VOS sentences the object asymmetrically c-commands the subject.

5. The discussion in section 3.7 is compatible with this as long as this abstract head A does not count as being the highest element of a chain.

6. See Kayne 1989b; 1991. There I proposed that apparent instances of a clitic adjoining to the right (e.g., of an infinitive, in Italian) are better analyzed as left-adjunction of the clitic to an abstract functional head, plus movement of the infinitive past the clitic. Another possibility, which I will not pursue here, would be for the infinitive to left-adjoin to the clitic. For relevant discussion, see Benincà and Cinque 1990.

Similar considerations hold for Romance subject clitic inversion, which might involve left-adjunction of the finite verb to the subject clitic.

7. Anderson (1992, p. 40) objects that Williams's proposal would incorrectly allow category changing via right-adjunction. Since the LCA-based theory I am developing here does not admit right-adjunction at all, this objection does not carry over.

8. Recall from section 3.3 that more than one adjunction to a given head is not permissible. Hence, it would not be possible to take *turn* to be adjoined to *-s* and *over* to be adjoined to *turns* (i.e., to *-s*).

9. Anderson (1992, p. 312) notes apparent counterexamples of the type *bejewel*, *deflea*, *enthrone*. The prefixes in these examples, though, are arguably incorporated particles (see, for example, the proposal concerning *be-* discussed in Mulder 1992, p. 178) and from my perspective, then, definitely not heads of W. The right-hand nominal morpheme presumably has the same status as in Hale and Keyser's (1993) analysis of (i), involving noun incorporation to an abstract V, which is the head.

(i) John will shelve the book.

10. The question of bracketing paradoxes is beyond the scope of this monograph. For relevant discussion, see Bok-Bennema 1994.

   For relevant discussion of morphology of the Arabic type, see Benmamoun and Vergnaud 1994.

11. This compound noun can be followed by an adjective (phrase), which could potentially play the role of S in (9). The solution is to treat such adjective phrases as being reduced relative clauses; on which, see section 8.4.

   There is at least one type of English compound noun that can cooccur with a complement.

(i) John's putdown(s) of Bill

This appears to match (9) closely and would therefore be expected to be ungrammatical under the strong interpretation of the LCA applying to subword structure that I have been entertaining in this section. It may be that (i), too, is a reduced relative, given (ii).

(ii) Those putdowns were all of Bill.

   Note that compounds such as (12) do not fall under the scope of (11). Nor, probably, does *putdown*, in particular if the internal structure is '$[_N[_V$ put] $[_{PP} [_P$ down]]]'.

12. Similar considerations hold for English *John often speaks of you*, and the like.

   Sentences with two preverbal clitics pose no new problems if the two clitics form a constituent, as discussed above for (9) of chapter 3. (Note that such a constituent as *me lo* 'me$_{DAT}$ it' in Italian must have the further structure '[[me l'] o]', to avoid having multiple adjunction to *-o*.)

   If two preverbal clitics are adjoined to separate functional heads, then exclusion of an adverb between them would require either dense stepwise movement of the subject DP or else movement of a phrase matching the second clitic, in the manner of Sportiche (1992), whose proposals about clitics mine are fairly close to.

13. I am setting aside here the question of left-dislocations.

Burridge (1983) claims that the Dutch preverbal negative clitic stopped appearing in root clauses as Dutch became strictly verb-second. If so, then this negative morpheme should be considered to have the same property attributed in the text to pronominal clitics. That is, it must not be able to adjoin to the finite verb; instead, it must only be able to adjoin to (or to occupy) a separate head position.

14. It seems clear that the clitic is not in C^0 either.

15. I am assuming that *Jean* here can only be in the specifier position just below C^0. For the subject to be lower than that, an empty category in subject position must be licensed. In French that is possible in "stylistic inversion" contexts (see Kayne 1980; 1986).

(i) Où   est Jean?
    where is Jean

In Italian and other Romance pro-drop languages an empty category in subject position is more widely possible.

The inversion seen in (23), although not involving the raising of the finite V to C, presumably does involve the raising of V to some intermediate position— possibly left-adjoining to the subject clitic itself. For further discussion, see Sportiche, n.d.

16. See Chomsky 1991 on the deletion in LF of (the trace of) Agr.

17. This conclusion is not compatible with Rizzi's (1991) way of extending the *wh*-Criterion to Romance inversion constructions.

18. If the verb in (26) moves instead to a functional head just below C^0, as proposed by Laka (1990) and Zanuttini (to appear), then the normal position of Romance clitics must be below that projection.

19. In Kayne 1991 I took that landing site to be adjunction to T′, which is not compatible with the conclusion of section 3.7 above. The alternatives are (1) adjunction of the infinitive to the clitic, which would recall proposals by Benincà and Cinque (1990) and (for Semitic, but specifically not for Romance, clitics) Shlonsky (1994) and Roberts and Shlonsky (1994), and (2) adjunction (or substitution) of the infinitive to a functional head higher than that to which the clitic is adjoined, as proposed by Belletti (1990) and Rooryck (1992). Either alternative requires rethinking section 2 of Kayne 1991, as does the next to last paragraph of note 16 of chapter 5. For an interesting proposal concerning the licensing of *if*, see Rooryck 1992, p. 247.

Chapter 5

1. Nor can the complex word orders of languages like Chinese and Kpelle be partially dependent on a directionality setting, as in Travis 1989.

2. Movement to a c-commanding but not asymmetrically c-commanding position is never possible under the present theory, most clearly if movement is copying, since the two copies would violate antisymmetry (each would asymmetrically c-command the subparts of the other).

3. I leave open the question of what drives all these movements (Case will certainly be at issue in some). For some interesting proposals on what might trigger the movements that make Dutch OV, see Zwart, to appear, and Koster 1993.

   In the case of DP complements, the movement that positions the O to the left of V in an OV language could be thought of as significantly akin to "scrambling." This might contribute to an understanding of why what has been called scrambling in the literature is more generally found in OV languages than in VO languages.

4. Compare the observation by Marácz (1989, p. 362n.) that P-DP order is possible in Hungarian only when the adposition in question is of the class that never shows agreement.

5. Thinking of agreement here in terms of a separate Agr node would not affect the argument.

6. Adposition raising, with an overt copy left behind, might underlie Spanish *conmigo*; in other words, this might well be, even synchronically, 'with-me-with'.

7. In Den Besten's (1977) influential proposal the finite verb moves to C^0. The text discussion is independent of the label of that position.

8. It is also essential to rule out derivations involving leftward movement of the finite verb to C^0, followed by leftward movement only in root contexts of IP to Spec,CP. (This kind of derivation might be impossible by virtue of the fact that the trace of the finite verb in IP would be unbound. Assuming such a headless IP not to be operator-like, reconstruction would be prohibited by Frank, Lee, and Rambow's (1991, p. 152) generalization that reconstruction for binding purposes is permitted only from operator positions; see note 24 of chapter 8.) The limitation to root contexts distinguishes this (illegitimate) case from that discussed by Nkemnji (1992) in which V raises leftward to a Neg^0, followed by the (successful) raising of VP to Spec,NegP.

9. This is incompatible with part of Laka's (1990) analysis of verb-complementizer interactions in Basque.

   Dutch has sometimes been analyzed as having rightward V-movement (of infinitives). From such a perspective, Dutch starts out with word order different from that of English. It then undoes this via rightward movement (which leaves open the question of why there are no mirror-image leftward V-movements of infinitives in the Germanic SVO languages), only to end up with a word order more like that of English. From the text perspective, on the other hand, Dutch starts out with English-like order, from which it departs via leftward movements. For further discussion, see Zwart, to appear.

   I agree with Everett's (1989) analysis of Yagua in terms of leftward V- and N-raising, while leaving open the question of how best to reconcile Yagua with Greenberg's (1966) Universal 33.

10. I have formulated this discussion in terms of incorporation of one head to another. Since what is crucially at stake is just the question of head raising, incorporation could be replaced by "checking by raising" in Chomsky's (1993) sense without the core of the discussion being affected.

11. In Chomsky's (1993) terms, one would say that person agreement is necessarily "strong."

12. In this discussion I am abstracting away from the additional movement of the verb that characterizes verb-second constructions.

13. See Haegeman and Zanuttini 1991 and Haegeman 1994.

The text proposal leaves open the question of ordering among complements; see Haider 1992 for interesting discussion. Haider's analysis has in common with mine the desire to reduce the range of phrase structure variation, even though the specifics seem on the whole incompatible. Haider argues that the neutral order among complements in German is the same as in English. (Note that dative-accusative order also holds for leftward-moved quantifiers in French (see Kayne 1975, sec. 2.14), in a way that Haider's approach does not seem to be able to capture.) Ackema, Neeleman, and Weerman (1993) show that in some cases the neutral order of complement and adjunct in Dutch is the reverse of what it is in English.

14. The prediction is not as strong as it might be, for the reason that the derivation of constituent YX via head-to-head movement leaves open the question of how much "fusion," if any, to expect.

Note that from the perspective of the theory being developed here, *head-final* can only mean that the head in question is not followed by any *overt* material within its projection.

In addition, languages like Japanese must have covert heads that are not head-final (e.g., to accommodate subject DPs), if I am correct in claiming that multiple adjunction to a given phrase is prohibited. See also note 3 of chapter 6.

If Otani and Whitman (1991) are correct in arguing for V-raising in Japanese (their analysis is argued against by Hoji (1994)), then V-I in Japanese would not match Y-X in (3) and Japanese would, from my perspective, have to have leftward V-raising.

Whitman's (1994) proposal concerning Korean preverbal negation can be reconsidered as follows. Complements in Korean must move leftward past that negation, in a way perhaps comparable to West Flemish, mentioned in the preceding section.

15. A third approach, one that might be compatible with the theory developed here, would have final complementizers reflecting successive leftward head movement plus multiple leftward movement of all the nonhead subparts of IP. On the other hand, such an approach might be excluded by the absence of sufficient functional heads to host the moved phrases to the left of C^0.

16. Note that from this perspective, the blocking effect of English *that* and similar complementizers in other languages probably cannot be stated in terms of obligatory head government as in Rizzi 1990b; see Frampton 1991.

Note further that if subjects originate within VP, then the ungrammaticality of (i) might be thought of as akin to a *that*-trace effect, with *to* playing the blocking role of *that*.

(i) *John to leave now would be a mistake.

One would then say that LF raising of *to* to *for* or to an exceptional Case-marking (ECM) or raising verb (see, in part, Baker 1988a, p. 489) neutralizes the violation. For French, one might say that the infinitival suffix *-r* plays the role of *to*, but that *-r* cannot incorporate in parallel fashion because *-r* is not prepositional (see, in part, Kayne 1981b). (Something further would need to be said about 'seem' in French.) Apparent cases of infinitival subjects in certain *wh*-constructions would be treated largely along the lines proposed by Pollock (1985). In agreement with Baltin (1993), PRO would be considered not to have raised past *to*.

This approach to (i) would lead to the expectation that a language that had a counterpart of *to*/*-r*, but in which that I^0 was final (i.e., in which the complement of that I^0 moved up to specifier position), would allow the equivalent of (i).

17. See Steever 1987, p. 739, and Krishnamurti and Gwynn 1985, p. 137.

Consideration of strongly head-final languages with subject-verb agreement calls into question some or much of Kuroda 1988.

18. If Chinese has a covert declarative C^0, then it must be a final C^0.

19. On the other hand, Marathi *aapaṇ* can be a nominative subject preceded by *ki* according to Wali and Subbarao (1991, p. 1096). Either they are right in claiming that *aapaṇ* is not an anaphor, or else *aapaṇ* must have a way of evading the blocking effect of *ki;* compare the fact that *that*-trace effects can be evaded even in certain varieties of English, as discussed by Sobin (1987).

The absence of nominative (and certain genitive) reflexives in Turkish (see George and Kornfilt 1981) might have to do with their not being monomorphemic (see Pica 1987), contrary to those discussed in the text (if so, then English *himself* is not directly relevant).

20. This is an oversimplification, given languages like Hungarian and in a more general way those discussed by Bhatt and Yoon (1992).

21. Huang's (1982) proposal for LF *wh*-movement in Chinese (and, by extension, in other *wh*-in-situ languages) raises the question of what the landing site could be. Conceivably, reconstruction makes one available that was not available in the overt syntax. Aoun and Li's (1993) proposal for empty operator movement in Chinese raises the same question. Perhaps there is an initial C'^0 in these languages that only licenses an empty operator, much like infinitival inflection licenses only an empty DP in many languages.

22. Imbabura Quechua is a largely head-final language that has obligatory *wh*-movement to clause-initial position; Hermon (1985, p. 36) observes that a question marker is suffixed to the *wh*-phrase. As Luigi Rizzi (personal communication) has pointed out, this question marker might be an overt initial C^0, confirming that movement of IP to Spec,CP has not taken place. See Hermon's (p. 146) own assumption that Comp (in present terms, C^0) is to the left (of the overt IP).

In root *wh*-questions in Vata (see Koopman 1984, pp. 35, 89) the *wh*-phrase is initial; they also have a clause-final element *la* that the text proposal must analyze as not being the head of the projection in whose specifier the *wh*-phrase is found. The head whose specifier does contain the *wh*-phrase must have an unmoved complement.

Somewhat similar to Quechua is Kamaiurá, as discussed by Brandon and Seki (1981), with preposing of interrogative words, yet with final complementizers and relativizers. These will be final heads (i.e., heads whose complements have moved leftward past them); interrogative words will be in the specifier of a head (perhaps the empty counterpart of the overtly initial yes-no particle) whose complement has not raised past it.

On the fact that languages display less internal cross-categorial uniformity with respect to the head-complement relation than is commonly thought, see the last paragraphs of note 14.

Chapter 6

1. That is, in (largely) head-final languages, in the sense of *head-final* determined by the present theory.

2. The alternative would be to take *et Paul* to be in the specifier of the second *et*. This kind of structure seems more plausible, though, for English *both, either, neither*; for example, in *both John and Bill* it might be that *both John* is in the specifier of *and*, with a kind of spec-head agreement between *both* and *and* licensing *both*.

3. See the third paragraph of note 14 of chapter 5. The possibility that Japanese (and similarly Korean) could have some overt heads whose overt complements follow them should be considered for *wa, ga* (and *o*) as well. A sentence of the form 'John ga Bill o . . .' would then be represented as follows:

(i) [John [ga [Bill [o . . .]]]]

If *wa* had the property that its specifier must be filled, then we would have an explanation for the absence of (ii).

(ii) *DP ga wa . . .

Since 'DP ga' is not a phrase under this hypothesis, *wa* would have nothing in its specifier.

The preceding analysis of *wa, ga* (and perhaps *o*) was suggested to me by Brody's (1990, p. 116) comparable proposal for Hungarian *is* 'also'. Also see Anderson's (1984) discussion of Kwakwala Case markers, which are phrase-initial syntactically but then cliticize onto the preceding word.

Carlson (1983, pp. 80ff.) discusses the fact that the Latin coordinating conjunction *-que* is cliticized to the first word of the second conjunct (when there are two conjuncts). This can be reinterpreted as follows: starting from '[XP [que YP]]', an initial head within YP moves out of YP and left-adjoins to *que*.

Carlson states that if the first word of the relevant conjunct is a monosyllabic preposition, then *que* cliticizes to the second word. From the perspective of the preceding paragraph, this should be reinterpreted as follows: a monosyllabic preposition + following word (e.g., demonstrative, with the preposition left-adjoined to it) can move leftward as a single head constituent, left-adjoining to *que* (and stranding the noun, in that case). (It may be that *monosyllabic preposition* here is related to the distinction in French between *à* 'to/at' and *contre* 'against' noted by Obenauer (1976, pp. 11ff.) to hold for leftward movement of P +

combien 'how much/many'; also see Kayne 1981a, sec. 1.2.) As for how these prepositions come to be left-adjoined to a demonstrative X^0, it may be appropriate to think of them as the spelling out of Case; see Vergnaud 1974, chap. 3, n. 35.

4. Postal (1993) argues plausibly that parasitic gaps cannot be taken to be a subcase of ATB extractions. The facts he adduces may, however, be compatible with Munn's position, if the extra restrictions observed with parasitic gaps can be attributed to the presence of an extra intervening *wh*-phrase or element like *without* or *before*, not present in ATB constructions.

5. Indirectly relevant here is the general question of whether sentential coordination and DP coordination are exactly parallel. The former perhaps more readily allows (the equivalent of) *and* not to appear, in some languages; see Payne 1985, p. 25. (Notable in English is *They went, the one to Paris, the other to London*, which deserves more study; concerning French, see Kayne 1975, sec. 1.9.) It may be that adverbial adjuncts can sometimes be used with the effect of coordination. (Examples might be *the pool that he went to the hotel and jumped into* versus **the pool into which he went to the hotel and jumped*, recalling extraction from adjuncts; see Chomsky 1982, p. 72, citing an observation by Adriana Belletti.)

Of relevance here is the question of what category is being coordinated in sentential coordination. Godard's (1989, p. 500) facts concerning the obligatory repetition of complementizer *que* in French could be taken to indicate that IP-coordination is not (readily) available.

6. I leave open the question of how best to express the fact that RNR extends to these clitic cases only marginally. Benincà and Cinque (1990) give Romanian examples, too, but note that the corresponding Italian examples are sharply ungrammatical. Sportiche (n.d.) states that such examples are better with disjunction than with conjunction, giving the example in (i).

(i) ?Pierre le   ou les   verra   au   concert.
    Pierre him or them will-see at-the concert

7. The conclusion reached in section 3.7 that heads cannot be specifiers will exclude '[Cl [and DP$_{lex}$]]'.

8. The landing site of the moved determiner must be low enough that the finite verb can move past it, but not so low that adverbs could intervene between it and the landing site of the finite verb. That a finite verb can move past a clitic is supported by certain root constructions in Portuguese and Galician, and more generally by the northern Italian dialect spoken in Borgomanero, where the finite verb precedes object clitics and can be separated from them by various elements, including the postverbal negation and nonclitic subject pronouns. For example:

(i) i dis mévvi 'subject-clitic$_{1SG}$ say I (cf. French *moi*) you$_{DAT.CLITIC}$ (cf. Italian *vi*)'

The example, one of many, is from Colombo 1967, p. 55.

9. Similarly for *John (repeatedly) ran up and (then) down the stairs*.

He pulled the lever up and (then) down should be taken to be comparable to *He pulled the cat off the table and (then) onto his lap*, with XP-coordination.

10. Dougherty's (1971, p. 307) example *hem and haw* must now be seen as an instance of VP-coordination, and not V-coordination.

11. As suggested in essence by McCloskey and Hale (1984, p. 524n.). Alternatively, there might be DP-coordination with an empty D^0 in the second DP. For relevant discussion, see Milner 1978, pp. 89ff.

Another candidate for head coordination is the repetitive coordination construction.

(i) John read and read and read.

But Lakoff and Peters (1969, p. 122n.) note the following example:

(ii) I hit him and hit him and hit him—until he died.

This shows that (i) can be taken to be an instance of XP-coordination. (That (i) and (ii) should be grouped together is supported by the fact that, for unclear reasons, the first *and* cannot be deleted in either, as they note; also see Gleitman 1969, p. 112.)

12. The fact that a clitic can be readily missing from the second conjunct if that conjunct is also missing an auxiliary is arguably a gapping effect.

(i) Jean vous   aurait   parlé   et   pardonné.
    Jean you$_{DAT}$ would-have spoken and forgiven
    'Jean would have spoken to you and forgiven you.'

This agrees with Kayne 1975, sec. 2.5, in taking the deletion of the clitic to be "parasitic" on the deletion of the auxiliary, but it differs in not taking (i) to bear directly on the question of whether clitic and auxiliary form a constituent. The reason is that gapping is known to be able to delete nonclitic complements along with the verb (see Kuno 1976 for a variety of examples).

13. In a sense that I will be unable to make precise. Benincà and Cinque (1990) note that, at least in Italian, the two verbs can differ in tense.

(i) Lo leggo e   leggerò   sempre con piacere.
    it I-read and will-read always with pleasure
    'I read it and always will read it with pleasure.'

(27) is more available in Spanish and Portuguese than in French or Italian; see Uriagereka 1988 and in particular Uriagereka's (1988; to appear) idea that Spanish and Portuguese clitics move past IP to a special F^0.

14. The ungrammaticality of (i) might be related to that of (ii).

(i) *For John with Bill would be fighting now.

(ii) *Mary wants very much for John with her tomorrow.

15. Thinking of Pesetsky 1995, one might claim that the empty head of the small clause must incorporate to the next category up, and that incorporation to a preposition is impossible, for reasons that remain to be elucidated. (An exception is the *with* of *With John sick, the family is in trouble.*) To extend to (47), this would require that *Bill with Paul* have an empty head, in other words, that *with* not be the highest head of that phrase.

The preposition restriction is also found in inalienable possession constructions like (i).

(i) The dog bit (*into) John on/in the leg.

This raises the possibility that *John on/in the leg* might be a subtype of coordinate constituent.

16. On this notion of (covert) distributor, see Heim, Lasnik, and May 1991.

The first *et* of (5) necessarily acts like a distributor, too; compare Payne's (1985, pp. 19–20) observation (in terms of his [+separate] feature) that the last *to* of (7) in Japanese does not have this property and that this is typical of final coordinate conjunctions. From the perspective of the LCA-based word order theory proposed here, it could be that a necessary condition for inducing an obligatory distributivity effect is that the conjunction in question asymmetrically c-command the other conjunctions within the phrase in question. In French '[et [DP [et DP]]]' the first *et* does asymmetrically c-command the second, whereas in Japanese '[[DP [to DP]]$_i$ [to [e$_i$]]]' neither *to* c-commands the other.

17. Perhaps relevant here is the blocking effect of *both* in (i).

(i) I consider (*both) John to have made a mistake and Bill to have participated in the cover-up.

18. *With* presumably Case-licenses its own complement *Bill* in (55), without assigning a theta-role to it (rather, *John with Bill* receives a theta-role from *friends*, with each conjunct interpreted in parallel fashion; see Munn 1993 for relevant discussion). In this respect, the *with* of coordination recalls Baker's (1988a, p. 300; 1988b) claim, which goes back through work by Marantz (1984, p. 246) to a proposal by Dick Carter, that the instrumental preposition plays no role in theta-assignment, which leads me to the following suggestion, namely, that a sentence like (i) derives from a structure like (ii),

(i) The boy broke the window with a hammer.

(ii) ... [the boy [with a hammer]] ...

in which the instrument and the subject form a subvariety of coordinate constituent with *with*. This would make it clearer why instrumentals are not theta-dependent on the preposition and would cast new light on why instrumentals can sometimes be superficial subjects, as in (iii).

(iii) The hammer broke the window.

The significance of the similarity between instrumental *with* and the *with* of coordination was in essence noted by Marantz (1984, pp. 247–248), who did not, however, propose (ii).

19. This is supported by a contrast brought to my attention by Paul Portner (personal communication).

(i) Mary bought but John didn't buy any books about linguistics.

(ii) *Mary didn't buy but John did buy any books about linguistics.

Negative polarity *any* can be licensed by a negation in the second, but not in the first, conjunct.

Postal (n.d.) argues that RNR forms a natural class with leftward extractions. If so, then (57) and (i) should involve abstract leftward movement of either the empty object in the first conjunct or the lexical object in the second (at LF) or both.

Chapter 7

1. On the other hand, the theory does not automatically tell us whether to take the head to be *to* or rather to be a V position, as suggested by Larson (1988). If the latter, the question arises whether some language could differ from English and fail to raise that V at all.

The derived structure proposed by Larson for (i) is not compatible with the present theory, since his derived structure involves right-adjunction of *a book*.

(i) Mary gave John a book.

Rather, '[John a book]' must correspond to a (headed) small clause, with *John* perhaps raising up to its surface position from a lower position that is within the small clause and below *a book*.

The grammaticality of *the gift of a book to Bill*, which led me in Kayne 1981c not to include (1) in the small clause approach to multiple complements, must now be accounted for otherwise; a promising proposal is that of Pesetsky (1995), in terms of how derived nominals are affected by constraints on zero-incorporation.

Zero-incorporation in Pesetsky's sense might also play a role in the following contrast:

(ii)   the person who we gave a picture of to the child

(iii)   *the person who we gave a picture of a new frame

2. It is to be noted that the LCA by itself does not exclude the possibility that in (3) there is a phrase *John criticized Bill* that is left-adjoined to/in the specifier of the phrase headed by *after*. Although I do not think it is appropriate here, I will suggest that kind of structure in section 9.2 for certain comparatives and resultatives.

3. Gross (1968, p. 136) gives one example with a direct object.

(i) Jean l'avertit   y   être allé.
    Jean her informed there to-be gone
    'Jean informed her that he'd gone there.'

This example also bears on the question of whether and how French infinitives might need Case; see Raposo 1987.

4. Left open is the question of why the two types of infinitive should differ in this way. With respect to LF movement of PRO in (4), recall the claim made in Kayne 1991, p. 679, to the effect that all instances of PRO are governed at LF. (The idea of (LF) movement of PRO was first suggested to me, in the context of that article, by Barbara Bevington.)

It is of note that in Corsican, to judge by observations of Yvia Croce (1979, p. 150), (5) itself is less good than the same sentence with a subjunctive instead of the infinitive, suggesting that in some languages PRO might be limited to subject orientation to a greater extent than in French.

Contrasting with (4) is (i).

(i) Il me semble avoir   mal   compris.
    it me seems   to-have wrong understood
    'It seems to me that I (must) have misunderstood.'

Here, where the matrix subject is an expletive, object control is possible, as if the dative object of *sembler* could itself move to subject position at LF.

Why French indicative-like infinitives are incompatible with *de* (on which, see note 34 of chapter 3), as opposed to their Italian counterparts, is unclear.

In both French and Italian (as opposed to Spanish), object control as in (5) requires *de* (with the exception, again with an expletive subject, of (ii)) for reasons that are unclear.

(ii) Il me faut partir.
     it me must to-leave
     'I must leave.'

If raising of PRO (which could take place prior to LF) were blocked by *if* but compatible with *whether* (in the presence of a *wh*-phrase, PRO would (first) move to C^0; see Borer 1989), one would have an alternative account of the control facts discussed in Kayne 1991, sec. 2. French *si* would act exactly like its English counterpart *if* (and similarly for the other Romance clitic-infinitive languages). In Italian (and the other infinitive-clitic Romance languages), the infinitive would move to a position higher than PRO and license long movement of it, much as in Rizzi's (1982, chap. IV) original analysis of Italian *wh*-movement. (On a link between "free inversion" and infinitive-clitic order, see Kayne 1991, p. 657.) The present paragraph may or may not be compatible with note 16 of chapter 5.

5. As suggested by Cinque (1993a, p. 266). Also see Ordóñez's (1994) proposal that Spanish VOS and German OSV structures share a common scrambling operation. Larson's idea that in (11) the '[V PP]' constituent moves leftward past the object DP would be compatible with the LCA if the landing site were a specifier position (of a head situated above the object). Although I will not pursue this possibility for English, a somewhat comparable movement of a verb-initial constituent into a high specifier position has been proposed with notable results for Irish by Duffield (1994).

6. I leave open the question of whether the verb should be taken to originate in Y^0, as in Larson's work, or whether X^0 and Y^0 should be taken to be nonverbal heads, as in Pesetsky 1995.

7. See, for example, Wexler and Culicover 1980, p. 278.

8. I find the following kind of example better than (20):

(i) ?the woman that they were explaining to the husband of all the intricacies of
    a divorce settlement

This is unexpected from Larson's V'-reanalysis perspective. From a leftward PP-movement perspective, the improved status of (i) can be related to that of (ii) as compared with (32) below in the text.

(ii) ?the woman that we think that to the husband of they should explain everything

On the interaction between P-stranding and scrambling in Dutch, see Koster 1987, p. 181. Note further that the deviance of "heavy NP shift" in the English double object construction is now to be reinterpreted as the deviance of scrambling the direct object leftward across the indirect object.

(iii) *?John has given a present most of the children who wanted one.

We can now see a link between this and the fact that in Dutch comparable scrambling is also deviant—"??" for Zwart (1993, p. 303), for example.

9. Leftward PP-movement of a similar sort has been proposed for Italian by Belletti and Shlonsky (to appear). They also propose a rightward movement analysis for certain Italian sentences that is not compatible with the ban on right-adjunction that I have derived. From my perspective, it should turn out that sentences such as (i) can be attributed to leftward PP-movement, too.

(i)   Maria ha dato a Gianni un libro.
      Maria has given to Gianni a   book

(ii) *Maria ne ha dato a Gianni uno.
      Maria of-it has given to Gianni one

The fact that (ii) is not possible would then recall the following contrast:

(iii) ?For his birthday, Mary gave to John a book.

(iv) *For his birthday, Mary gave to John one.

A Gianni in (i) may have raised higher than *to John* has raised in (iii). Correspondingly, *un libro* in (i) may be higher than *a book* in (iii), thereby accounting for the full acceptability of the Italian example. (These differences would be related to the fact that verbs raise higher in Italian than in English; see Belletti 1990.)

10. Contrary to Chomsky (1993), but in the spirit of Johnson (1991) and Koizumi (1993).

On the position of object pronouns in Irish, generally more to the right than expected (see O Siadhail 1989, p. 207), see Duffield 1994.

11. It may now be possible to take the surface position of the adverb in (i) to be due to leftward movement from a postobject position, with implications for head movement.

(i) John carefully undid the package.

A clear case of leftward adverb movement to other than sentence-initial position is found in French.

(ii) J'ai mal dû   raccrocher.
     I have wrong must hang-up
     'I must have hung up wrong.'

This leftward movement resembles that of French *tout* 'everything' and *rien* 'nothing' discussed in Kayne 1975, chap. 1.

Given the ban on movement of a single-bar-level category (i.e., of a single segment of a two-segment category; recall the end of section 3.1), it follows that the movement of the *to*-phrase in (iii) must strand some head (Y^0) intervening between it and the ECM subject.

(iii) John considers to be intelligent all the students in his class.

(iv) ... considers [[to be intelligent]$_i$ X^0 [[all ...] [Y^0 [e]$_i$ ...

Assuming that the ECM subject originates within the *to*-phrase (see note 16 of chapter 5), (iii) contrasts minimally with German (see Frank, Lee, and Rambow 1991)—perhaps because the *to*-phrase in (iii) is governed by V in a way that it is not in German.

12. Williams (1977, p. 130) gives (a sentence like) (27) a "*" and (one like) (26) a "?".

The idea that these involve extraction from VP (rightward) was proposed by Jayaseelan (1985).

13. There is a point in common here with Hornstein's (1994) proposal for LF movement to Spec,Agr$_0$.

14. A proposal for particle incorporation can be found in Van Riemsdijk 1978, p. 54. (Syntactic incorporation followed by excorporation of V may be appropriate for the Basque "light verb" constructions discussed by Laka (1993, p. 153).)

Johnson's (1991, p. 600) account of particle constructions in English is also compatible with the present theory, if his account is modified to start from '[$_V$ P + V]' prior to excorporation of V rather than from '[$_V$ V + P]'.

The line of research started by Guéron (1987), which adopts the small clause approach to particle constructions but takes *the book* in (33) to be complement of the particle, also seems compatible. For recent development of that approach (which may not require excorporation—an advantage, given (the text to) note 6 of chapter 3) and careful discussion of the complexities of particle constructions with two DPs, see den Dikken 1992.

We will see in section 9.1 that sentences like (i) indicate that *a book* must in fact originate below the surface position of the particle.

(i) John picked a book up that had fallen.

15. We might then expect Italian to allow VSO sentences, and in fact (i) is grammatical, albeit with a special intonation (roughly speaking, rising on the subject and falling on the object) that led Antinucci and Cinque (1977) to give it the name *emarginazione*.

(i) Ha scritto Gianni questo articolo.
    has written Gianni this   article
    'Gianni wrote this article.'

In the spirit of section 7.3, I take this special intonation to be compatible with the claim that *questo articolo* is asymmetrically c-commanded by *Gianni*.

On VOS sentences in Spanish, see Ordóñez 1994.

16. The idea that in the core cases of stylistic inversion like (36) the subject can be taken to be in a left-hand position goes back to Déprez 1988. On the other hand,

Déprez takes those cases of stylistic inversion that display '... verb-complement-subject' order to involve right-adjunction. I will take them instead to be instances of scrambling of the complement across a heavy subject, with the subject in a left-hand specifier position.

The impossibility of '... verb-subject-complement' order when the complement is a direct object remains to be understood. There may be a link with a comparable restriction on English quotative inversion (see Branigan and Collins 1993) and/or with a similar restriction on the English presentational *there*-construction.

The mixed possibilities of '... verb-subject-complement' order when the complement is a PP cannot be interpreted as in Kayne 1986, app. II, since that proposal (which left open the question of subjunctive contexts) depended on right-adjunction. Similarly, the restrictions discussed in Kayne 1981a, app., need to be rethought, perhaps in terms of LF movement of the postverbal subject.

17. A similar suggestion was made by Szabolcsi (to appear) for *Where did he go, do you think?* in terms of clausal pied-piping.

18. Unless (41) is an instance of movement, stranding the auxiliary, as in what is called VP-preposing, with the difference that in (41) the input structure would be less familiar.

(i) John is he is real smart

The doubling of the auxiliary would recall Chomsky's (1993, pp. 34ff.) proposal to interpret movement as involving copying. The relation between *John* and *he* might be assimilable to that of doubling, as discussed below.

19. This type of reduction is probably akin to that of (i).

(i) Mary's smart, but not John.

20. It may be that the construction discussed by Ronat (1982; 1984) should be interpreted as the French (near) equivalent of (47).

21. The fact that (52) is not possible with *Marie* substituted for *elle* (intonation kept constant) might be due to a higher position for the latter, if Koopman (1993a) is correct.

22. Italian differs here from French and Spanish, for reasons that remain to be discovered.

23. This account of (58) means that one no longer has to grapple with the problems caused by trying to extend Subjacency to rightward movements, nor is there any need to invoke a highly specific constraint such as Ross's (1967) Right Roof Constraint. This point will come up again with respect to "extrapositions" in chapter 9. See also the discussion of (14) of this chapter.

24. This is in part similar to proposals made by Iatridou (1991), who however agrees with Cinque in generating the left-dislocated phrase in its left-hand position in simple sentences.

Cinque demonstrates conclusively that CLLD is not a subcase of *wh*-movement. From the text perspective, *wh*-movement and CLLD differ in that the latter is not an instance of an operator-variable configuration at LF. Whether this will suffice to account for all the differences Cinque notes I leave an open question.

Cinque's (1990, p. 72) proposal for accounting for the obligatoriness of the clitic in the direct object subtype of CLLD seems orthogonal to the question of whether the empty category in complement position is base-generated or produced by (non-*wh*-)movement.

The fact that that clitic is obligatory in CLLD, but not in right-dislocation (cf. (47)), follows from the present theory as a result of the fact that the latter involves no movement of the lexical direct object.

Cinque (1990, pp. 57ff.) distinguishes CLLD from left-dislocation (LD). LD involves an initial DP that should be base-generated in a very high specifier position. The fact that there is no counterpart to LD with a final DP (i.e., no construction with the properties of LD holding of a final DP) follows from the absence of right-hand specifier or adjoined positions, under the present theory.

25. Overt CLLD allows more than one such landing site; see Cinque 1990, p. 58. The same is true of right-dislocation, that is, of covert CLLD.

Cinque (p. 59) notes that the resumptive element in Italian CLLD must be a pronominal clitic and cannot be a pronominal nonclitic. The same appears to be true of covert CLLD.

In French, as opposed to Italian, CLLD of a dative generally dispenses with the preposition, which is required in right-dislocation (in both languages).

(i) Ton ami, je lui   parle souvent.
     your friend I him$_{DAT}$ speak often

(ii) Je lui parle souvent, *(à) ton ami.

I assume that (i) can be a true case of CLLD (vs. what Cinque (p. 57) calls LD; also see Cinque 1977, p. 408n., and Benincà 1988b, p. 133), as suggested by the possibility of *ton ami* occurring noninitially (see Hirschbühler 1975, (31b)). The contrast between French and Italian concerning (i) is probably related to the fact that French dative quantifiers can do without *à* (see Kayne 1975, sec. 2.14)—a possibility that appears to be absent from Italian. (The positioning of those prepositionless dative quantifiers in French recalls that of Italian *loro* 'them', which Cardinaletti (1991) demonstrates to be outside of VP.)

26. Clitic doubling of the nondislocated type may involve LF movement of a type distinct from CLLD, for example, if the doubled phrase in (63) is negative (and if negative phrases move at LF; see Haegeman and Zanuttini 1991 and Longobardi 1992); see Dobrovie-Sorin 1990, p. 390.

LF movement of one or the other type may underlie the restrictions on intonational phrasing discussed by Hirst (1993).

27. Note that French allows *Jean la voit elle* 'Jean her sees her' without dislocation intonation, much as in (52). Similarly, Spanish allows *Juan la ve a ella*. The preceding French example differs slightly from its dative counterpart (see Kayne 1975, chap. 2, n. 41); this might indicate some link with the construction studied by Ronat (1979), *Elle me voit elle* 'she me sees she (= Shé sees me)'.

Note further that from the present perspective, the problem with (66) is not a Case problem, and that in (67) *Marie* presumably is Case-licensed as a nondoubled complement is.

28. On the other hand, no Romance language seems to allow locative clitics to evade (65). This is especially striking for languages llke Trentino, which, as Cordin (1990) notes, has nondislocated clitic doubling with dative clitics but not with locative clitics, even though locative and (third-person) dative clitics are homonymous.

29. In some varieties of Spanish (69) is grammatical with direct objects that take *a*. Given the second paragraph of note 27, the role of *a* in licensing (69) cannot readily be taken to be a Case role with respect to *María*.

An alternative view is that *a* in some way licenses the (partial) dativization of the apparently accusative clitic, so that (69) is assimilated to dative clitic doubling.

Chapter 8

1. See Bittner and Hale 1994 and Holmberg and Platzack, to appear, on the licensing of nominative by C^0.

2. On the relation of which to *one*, see Perlmutter 1970.

3. This recalls the fact that Hungarian focus and interrogative phrases move to a pre-V position that is below C^0.

4. Some speakers do not find this unacceptable; see Smith 1969, p. 254n. They presumably have the possibility of either an implicit relative (see below on the ameliorating effect of relatives) or use of a lower *the* (see the discussion of (35) of chapter 9).

5. This formulation, which implies that *'s* is not a D^0, does not by itself answer the question of why there is no DP recursion. Relevant here is the question of whether and to what extent there is CP recursion, given Szabolcsi's claim that C^0 and D^0 are parallel.

6. Also see Brame 1976, p. 125, and Schachter 1973. The use of DP and CP in the text version of the raising analysis draws on developments subsequent to the seventies.

I agree with Schachter's point that clefts are parallel to relatives. In the present framework the analysis of clefts should be as follows. Like relatives, clefts involve movement to Spec,CP. Unlike the CP of relatives, the CP of clefts is not the complement of D^0, but the complement of *be*.

(i)   It is CP

(ii) It is [$_{CP}$ linguistics$_i$ [that [we are studying [e]$_i$ ...

(It is not clear whether clefts with *wh*-words are like (ii) (with a generalization of the analysis of *wh*-words given below) or instead a subvariety of right-dislocation.)

Savio (1991) proposes that what looks like a right-hand (postverbal) focus position in Tamil (which would be impossible under the present theory) is actually a position to the left of an invisible copula in a cleft construction (which is compatible with the present theory).

Tuller (1992) argues that postverbal focus positions in Chadic are actually left-adjunctions to VP (with V raised to I). On the other hand, her (p. 317) proposal that in some Chadic languages nonfocused direct objects right-adjoin to V must be reinterpreted in terms of a higher adjunction site (specifier position) for those direct objects than for focused phrases.

7. This '[$_{DP}$ D^0 CP]' structure, though without movement to Spec,CP, may find additional support in cases of sentential embedding with an initial determiner, as in the Italian definite article + infinitive phrase construction.

(i) l'aver   lui affermato ...
    the to-have he affirmed

See Rizzi 1982, p. 85.

8. See Baker 1988a, pp. 378, 453, on noun incorporation from within the subject of an ECM construction; in fact, the structural relation between *the* and NP in (10) is reminiscent of an ECM construction.

The Romanian example (11) is from Dobrovie-Sorin 1990; on the N-to-D raising, see specifically Dobrovie-Sorin 1987 and Cornilescu 1992.

9. Though there might be parallel N-to-D movement in LF (see Longobardi, to appear), as a way, for example, to check Case (that is morphologically on N) in languages like German or Hungarian.

10. Some indirect objects can have an empty preposition.

(i) la persona cui ho   dato un libro
    the person who I-have given a   book

For discussion of French/Italian *lequel*/*il quale* 'the which' and various complexities, see Kayne 1976 and Cinque 1982.

11. Pollock (1992, p. 142) gives an example like (17) three question marks.

12. See Emonds 1979, p. 221n. As Giuliana Giusti (personal communication) suggests, *who* could be taken to be a form of *which* that appears under spec-head agreement with a [+human] NP.

(i) [man$_i$ [who [e]$_i$]]

Note that the Romanian counterpart of (21) will now involve N-to-D raising out of the specifier of the specifier of the sister of D. See note 8, recalling in particular that specifiers are necessarily adjoined phrases, given the LCA.

13. This does not hold for what are often called "headless" relatives.

(i) We gave him what little money we had.

(ii) We'll take whichever seat you offer us.

On the text analysis, these instead differ in that the NP sister of the *wh*-determiner has not raised. (The terms *headed* and *headless* are inappropriate in any event, since what has standardly been referred to by the term *head of a relative* is really a phrase (NP), from the text perspective.) It seems plausible to claim that, at least in (ii), raising has taken place—but raising of *which*, starting from a structure in which *ever* is a kind of determiner (regarding interpretation, see Larson 1987, p. 257).

(iii) ever [which seat [you offer us [e]]]

Left-adjunction of *which* to *ever* here would then recall the N-to-D raising in Romanian mentioned earlier.

Note the following contrast:

(iv)   However many people one speaks to, it's never enough.

(v)   *?To however many people one speaks, it's never enough.

If acceptable to some speakers, (v) is comparable to the Latin and French examples discussed in the last paragraph of note 3 of chapter 6.

14. See Kayne 1975, sec. 5.3, and Belletti 1982. Belletti's (p. 102) example

(i)   ... hanno   criticato l'uno   le   idee dell'altro.
       they-have criticized the one the ideas of-the other

could indicate that the specifier of the definite article is unavailable in Italian only when the head N is reciprocal *altro;* or perhaps in this kind of example *l'uno* can be in the specifier of a functional head external to the *le*-phrase.

15. The fact that in Russian the *wh*-word shows the Case determined by the lower predicate and the "head noun" the Case of the upper can be accounted for as follows. In *which picture* Case is assigned/licensed within the embedded sentence to *which*. In Russian, if *picture* remains as complement to *which* (in a nonrelative structure), an additional mechanism copies/licenses the same Case on *picture*. If *picture* moves to Spec,*which*, then it is Case-licensed in Spec,CP via the upper D^0 instead.

The structure in (29) but without the initial D^0 (see (i) of note 6) may be appropriate for the German counterpart to clitic left-dislocation (see section 7.3).

(i) Den Mann, den haben wir nicht gesehen.
    the man   him have we not   seen

Since '[den Mann$_i$ [den [e]$_i$]]' would be a single constituent, (i) would then no longer be an exception to the verb-second requirement of German.

16. The approach taken in Kayne 1983b, sec. 3.3, depended on a characterization of *wh*-phrases that is not in the spirit of section 3.5 above. LF movement of *who* in (33) might be a viable alternative (see Safir 1986, pp. 680–681), depending on the exact status of island violations in LF movement constructions.

From the text perspective, (i) is a movement-based parasitic gap construction.

(i)   ?the man whose wife's love for whom knows no bounds

The following seems to be less deviant than might be expected (cf. a partially similar example in Safir 1986, n. 18):

(ii)   ??This is the book that I would like very much for which to be sent to me.

It is a kind of relative *wh*-in-situ, with *book* moving from the complement of which to Spec,CP (perhaps via Spec,*which*) without the *which*-phrase itself having moved to Spec,CP. That movement of *book* is involved is supported by the stronger deviance of (iii).

(iii)   *This is the book that I insist that which should be sent to me.

17. In the only alternative configurationally permitted by the LCA, the relative clause would be a complement of N^0.

18. An alternative might be to say that LF movement of *book* to *the* (see note 9) is somehow blocked by *that* when *book* is in the specifier of another phrase within Spec,CP. This formulation would not extend to interrogatives, but it would correctly distinguish relatives from concessives in standard French.

(i) *la fille à qui que tu parles
     the girl to who that you speak

(ii) A qui que tu parles,...
     to who that you speak
     'No matter who you speak to,...'

(The concessive in (ii) might involve left-adjunction of *à qui* to *que* as with English *ever* in note 13, with French being more like Latin than English is.)

Obligatory LF N-to-D movement might provide the means to exclude (iii).

(iii) *Chair on which were you sitting?

The idea would be that the moved NP complement of *which* must be licensed in Spec,PP by a governing D^0.

Conversely, the relativized NP that comes to be governed by D^0 can bind an empty category within Spec,CP only if that empty category is governed by a *wh*-word.

(iv) the chair$_i$ on which [e]$_i$ he was sitting

(v) *the chair on [e]i (that) he was sitting

19. The ungrammaticality of (36) was noted by Jespersen (1974, sec. 4.5_2).

20. However, I find both (36) and (35) improved if the subject of the relative clause introduced by the null C^0 is pronominal.

(i) I just read the book about your ancestors you published last year.

(ii) ?I just read the book that's about your ancestors you gave me last year.

This suggests that a pronominal subject in English can cliticize to a null C^0 and render it (partly) immune to the text effect.

This recalls the phenomenon described by Giacomo-Marcellesi (1978, p. 212) for (mostly southern) Corsican, whereby a missing complementizer is licensed by an initial subject pronoun (also see Culioli 1981).

In addition, Cinque (1981, p. 298n.) gives the following examples:

(iii) Non sapevo tu   fossi malato.
      NEG I-knew you$_{NOM}$ were sick

(iv) *?Non sapevo Giorgio fosse malato.

This suggests that a cliticized subject pronoun can contribute to the licensing of subjunctive null complementizers in Italian (but not in Spanish; see Torrego 1983, n. 2).

For me this effect is also present with relative clause "extraposition" (on which, see section 9.1).

(v) ?A book just came out I've been meaning to read.

(vi) *?A book just came out my wife's been meaning to read.

Similarly:

(vii)   ?The fact it's out now is what's important.

(viii) *?The fact your book's out now is what's important.

On the other hand, there is no such effect with sentential subjects, indicating that the unification of all these English cases envisaged in Kayne 1981a, n. 23, and Stowell 1981 was not entirely correct.

(ix) *(That) it's out now is wonderful.

21. In (i) the italicized phrase in the specifier of the null complementizer has a complement, but that complement (*book that's about vour ancestors*) has moved to specifier position (of *which*), thereby evading the restriction.

(i) I just read the *book that's about your ancestors which* your son gave me last year.

22. On the lack of relative pronouns in N-final cases, see Downing 1978, pp. 392–394, and Keenan 1985, p. 149. On the lack of relative and sentential complementizer identity in N-final cases, see Keenan 1985, p. 160.

23. If a relative CP raises to Spec,DP and NP raises within CP to Spec,CP, the result is the Yoruba type of relative illustrated by Keenan (1985, p. 145). If N-to-D raising is general in relatives (see note 18), then in Yoruba it must take place under "reconstruction" (see Chomsky 1993).

24. Amharic has an element *ya*, which Gragg calls a relative particle, that precedes the verb within the relative clause. The text proposal implies that *ya* cannot be a C^0. It may rather be an I^0 past which at least the complements of V have raised, perhaps in a way similar to what transpires in Dutch or German; see section 5.4.

   Similarly, in languages where a relative particle follows the relative proper and precedes N (or D), that relative particle cannot be C^0, but only some kind of I^0 (whose complement has raised to its specifier).

   Note further that in (41) IP contains the trace resulting from the movement of NP to Spec,CP, and that subsequent to the movement of IP to Spec,DP that NP trace is not c-commanded by its antecedent. For interesting discussion of how to distinguish legitimate from illegitimate cases of traces being raised past their antecdents, see Muller 1994. One legitimate case is that of German "remnant topicalization," as studied by Den Besten and Webelhuth (1990).

   Concerning IP-movement to Spec,DP, minimality requirements could be met as in Chomsky 1993 by abstract incorporation of C^0 to D^0 (see note 16 of chapter 5), though overt incorporation of (the equivalent of) *that* to D^0 is evidently prohibited, as is incorporation of *that* to other categories, for unclear reasons.

25. NP could not be stranded in Spec,CP by leftward movement of the constituent '[C^0 IP]', since that constituent corresponds to just the lower segment of the category CP, and isolated segments (i.e., single-bar categories in more usual X-bar terms) cannot be moved (recall the last two paragraphs of section 3.1).

26. The relative unity of UG relativization appears to be supported by de Rijk's (1972, p. 121) observation in Basque N-final relatives of matching effects of the

sort often found in N-initial relatives; for some recent discussion of matching effects in the latter, see Larson 1987.

Note on the other hand, that what moves to the relative Spec,CP is not always NP (see (29)). (An indefinite) DP is also what moves to Spec,CP in (7), given the analysis of possessives proposed in section 8.1. Impossible would be a definite DP in the relative Spec,CP under *the*; see Williamson 1987, p. 175.

27. In some languages (e.g., Basque; de Rijk 1972) N in (42) can raise and left-adjoin to D^0.

28. On I-to-C movement, see Pesetsky 1982. Recall, in this regard, the argument given in section 4.6 to the effect that Romance clitics adjoin not to finite V but to a higher abstract head. Thus, for the I-to-C movement in the text, I could be this abstract head (stranding the clitic, if one is present). (The IP that raises in (42) is the category sister to C^0.)

29. There remains the question of why no language seems to have the structure '*IP–the–picture–which', which would result from moving IP in (43) to Spec,DP and leaving the rest untouched. It may be that there is a link to (i) (vs. *I don't know who to buy pictures of*).

(i) *Pictures of I don't know who to buy.

For example, it may be that from Chomsky's (1993) trace-as-copy perspective, the trace of *who* following *of* is uninterpretable, and similarly for the trace within the relative IP of *picture-which* (as opposed to the non-*wh* trace of *picture* alone in (42), which would be interpretable in situ).

30. I leave open the question of what forces NP-movement to Spec,CP to be overt, rather than LF, movement—for example, the question of what rules out the (attempted) relative in (i), with no overt movement to Spec,CP at all (and similarly for free relatives).

(i) *the [$_{CP}$[(that) [John bought (which) pictures

The relation between (49) and Condition C violations such as *He_i thinks $John_i$ is smart* needs to be elucidated.

Note that nothing prevents the existence in some language of the counterpart of (47) with (the equivalent of) *which picture* in place of *picture*; see the Bambara facts discussed by Schachter (1973, p. 35).

31. For example, if the mechanism proposed by Rizzi (1990b, pp. 66ff.) for allowing *the book that was sent to me* depended on Tense, which is lacking in (57).

A second possibility would be to invoke the general (but not very well understood) impossibility of having *that* with small clauses and infinitives (see Kayne 1991, n. 75); this would require distinguishing *that* from the French *de*, to be discussed below.

32. Spec,CP is thus assimilated in (57) to an A-position, a possibility dependent on the trace of *book* not being in a Case-marked position itself. This is presumably what is behind the lack of an ECP violation in (57), as opposed to the impossibility of *the book was sent to me* as a relative.

33. For recent discussion of PRO, see Chomsky and Lasnik 1993 and Kayne 1991.

34. In this pseudopassive example the perhaps abstractly incorporated preposition (see Baker 1988a, p. 260) must not count as part of an overt complement.

35. Contrary to the proposals of Bresnan (1982, p. 53) and others. Stronger evidence for adjectivalization comes from *unreferred to, unslept in;* whether this notion of adjectivalization is ultimately syntactic, or lexical, and in what sense, remains to be clarified.

36. Consider Cinque's (1993b) observation that stress in Italian can license a bare adjective in a position following a noun complement.

(i) la loro aggressione all'Albania,   BRUTALE
    the their aggression   against Albania brutal

I take this example to have essentially the representation given in the text for (57), with *aggressione all'Albania* in place of *book* and *brutale* in place of *sent to me.* (I leave open the question of where *loro* is attached.)

37. This CP can also occupy a lower position relative to *the.*

(i) the other recently arrived letter

This bears on the question of N-to-D incorporation that was relevant in the discussion of (58) and (60).

38. The idea of deriving adjectives from relatives is not new; see, for example, Smith 1969.

39. Recall that the covert equivalent of such raising was proposed earlier for English in the discussion of (58) and (60); also see notes 8 and 9.

40. Most of Romance is like French, but see Bernstein 1993 for a finer-grained analysis of N-raising based on Walloon.

41. On *-ci* and on *celui,* see Gross 1977, pp. 128ff., and on possessives, see Gragg's (1972, p. 160) point that the Amharic genitive construction is transparently related to relative clauses.

42. An adjective adjacent to *voiture* would presumably be part of the phrase moved from within IP to Spec,CP, except perhaps for the kind of elements mentioned in note 37.

Cinque (1993b) notes the contrast in Italian between (i) and (ii) (where *di Gianni* goes with *sostenitori,* not with *causa*).

(i)   i   sostenitori di Gianni fedeli   alla   causa
      the supporters of Gianni faithful to-the cause

(ii) *i sostenitori fedeli alla causa di Gianni

In (i) *fedeli alla causa* is a reduced relative, with *sostenitori di Gianni* in its Spec,CP, from the text perspective. In (ii), on the other hand, *sostenitori fedeli alla causa* is in Spec,*di,* in the sense of (79). Adapting Cinque's proposal for (ii), I can interpret it as violating the restriction against complex specifiers discussed above (see (62)), with *di/de* acting like empty C^0, rather than like *that* (for reasons that are unclear).

Note that, compared with (56), both (i) and the acceptable *the book of yours given to me by your son last year* (cf. also the only mildly deviant (36)) indicate that the core notion of "complex specifier" may involve "containing a complement with a nonnull IP."

43. There is another possessive construction in French (that is nonstandard with a definite article).

(i) la voiture à Jean
    the car   to Jean

I do not think that this *à* has the same syntactic status as *de*, in part for reasons discussed in Kayne 1975, sec. 2.20, in part because in Walloon both prepositions can be used together (see Remacle 1952, p. 342),

(ii) C'è d-à mîne.
     it is of to mine

and in part because of the contrast between (iii) and (iv).

(iii) la conférence d'hier
       the lecture   of yesterday

(iv) *la conférence à hier

44. The Case-licensing strategy used for *Jean* in (81), based on the presence of *de* in D/P^0, is evidently not workable in (82), either because of a problem with what would then have to be an expletive subject of BE, or because Case licensing via *de* requires the sister constituent of *Jean* to be empty. It may also be that the sister of I^0 cannot be interpreted in Spec,BE, an A-position. On the need for an indefinite article in (83), see perhaps Pollock's (1983) discussion of predicate nominals.

45. The fact that the IP sister to *de* is never finite recalls the comparable property of English *for*. This leads one to wonder about the claims made in Kayne 1991, pp. 667ff., concerning the status of the *de* that precedes infinitivals; see note 19 of chapter 4.

46. As a first approximation, this could be stated by saying that possessive I^0 must be '*s* (and cannot be abstract) when the possessor is human (apart from the relational cases alluded to).

An exception is when the possessor is heavy.

(i) (?)the car of the man I was telling you about

It seems that abstract possessive I^0 can be licensed in this context on the basis of its specifier being complex, in the sense of note 42.

Notice that (86) is excluded no matter what the initial determiner is.

(ii) *a car of John

This supports the (implicit) text claim that the exclusion of (86) is distinct from that of (103), given the well-formedness of *a car of John's*.

47. Although the text formulation does not imply it, a more careful study would probably lead to the conclusion that *that Paris* has a structure like (i),

(i) that [[THERE]$_j$ [C/D/P^0 [$_{IP}$ Paris I^0 [e]$_j$ . . .

where THERE is the abstract counterpart of the *there* found in the nonstandard English (ii).

(ii) that there book

See (the text to) note 41. A possible alternative to (i), modeled on (57), would be (iii).

(iii) that [Paris$_i$ [C/D/P^0 [$_{IP}$[e]$_i$ I^0 THERE...

This structure may be appropriate for another kind of example mentioned by Vergnaud (1974), namely, *the Mary with blue eyes.*

(iv) the [Mary$_i$ [C/D/P^0 [$_{IP}$[e]$_i$ I^0 [with blue eyes]...

The reason for the ungrammaticality of (v) remains to be discovered.

(v) *Mary is with blue eyes.

48. Like *ones* is Irish *té*, to judge by McCloskey 1979, p. 39.

49. I am assuming here that for thematic/interpretive reasons *from New Jersey* cannot be a complement of *students*. Consequently, (97) has no possible analysis as a double complement structure. A valid example of a double complement structure with a N^0 head would be (i).

(i) the theft of the money from the students

The two complements must form a small clause; this is different from the conclusion reached in Kayne 1981c, but consonant with Pesetsky 1995; also see section 7.1. (Each complement in (i) is within the minimal projection of *theft*, whereas *from New Jersey* in (99) is not within the minimal projection of ones.)

50. As seen in *the John's car*, in any event. The nonstandard (i) might reflect the licensing of covert *the* by the *'s* heading the specifier of the CP complement of that covert *the*.

(i) ?John's car that I was telling you about

51. Taking *de Jean/of John's* to be complements of *voiture/car* is not an option made available by UG; this is presumably related to the fact that an agent of V can be expressed as its subject, but not as its complement.

The analysis that I have proposed for French *la voiture de Jean* has left open the question of the apparent extractability of *de Jean*. For relevant discussion, see Cinque 1982, Giorgi and Longobardi 1991, and Pollock 1992.

For interesting restrictions on this extractability (in the case of French clitic *en* 'of it/them'), see Kupferman 1991, pp. 54–55.

52. The determiner and intonation aside, this construction recalls constructions in Chinese (see Li and Thompson 1981, p. 118) and Tagalog (see Schachter and Otanes 1972, p. 122), for which a comparable analysis should be considered.

On the French construction, see Kayne 1975, chap. 2, n. 55, Vinet 1977, and Milner 1978, p. 164.

53. That this construction could receive an analysis parallel to the one proposed in Kayne 1993 for English *a sweater of John's* and pursued here in sections 8.1 and 8.5 was suggested to me by Juan Uriagereka (personal communication; he also

suggested an extension to partitives, which I will leave unexplored). The construction in (107) has been studied for French by Milner (1978), Coursaget-Colmerauer (1975, pp. 21ff.), and Ruwet (1982).

54. *D'autre* here and in other ways acts differently from other *de*-AP phrases, as discussed by Huot (1981, pp. 276ff.).

55. See Huot's (1981, p. 261) claim that the *de* of *de*-AP is a complementizer.

The idea that *de* in (111) has *quelqu'un* within its maximal projection (and similarly for (112)/(113)) is proposed by Kupferman (to appear).

56. I take D^0 here to be empty/indefinite.

57. This recalls Rizzi 1990b, assuming that Relativized Minimality can be sensitive to category distinctions: A-movement of NP/AP across an intervening NP/AP in an A-position is blocked. But comparable movement to an Ā-position is allowed, and movement of NP to an A-position (nonoperator position) across an A-position DP is allowed. Left unaccounted for is why *de* matters, as it seems to, comparing the focalization in (105) with the absence of such an effect in (72).

Kupferman's (1991, p. 57) observation that (i) is impossible suggests that the Ā-movement in question is finely sensitive to category and cannot move a nominal category across another nominal category (nor, presumably, adjectival across adjectival).

(i) *quelqu'un de médecin
    someone of doctor

58. Unanswered here is why focal stress is needed in this case and not in the case of ordinary finite relatives with complementizer *que*. Perhaps there is some link to the fact about stress mentioned above concerning (66), and/or *que* has some licensing feature that *de* cannot have.

59. Note that the trace in question is the trace of *quel homme* within the DP *quel homme d'intelligent*. The trace within VP of the phrase *quel homme d'intelligent* is presumably properly licensed as a variable, by virtue of a special property of such *wh*-phrases when they are in Spec,CP. Further work is called for here.

60. I leave open whether (124) and (121) (without the clitic) can be excluded in the manner of note 57—and likewise, whether Cinque's binding theory approach could be generalized to exclude (114) and (119). Of potential importance also is Chomsky 1993.

61. Azoulay-Vicente (1985, pp. 29, 237) also gives examples showing that the AP following *de* cannot be complex in certain kinds of cases. Under the text analysis, where AP is in Spec,IP, it might be possible to link this to the restrictions on complex specifiers mentioned earlier; see (36).

Similarly, perhaps, for the fact that the NP in Spec,D/PP (i.e., the NP preceding *de*) can itself not contain *de*-AP or a relative clause; see Huot 1981, pp. 277–278.

62. Moro's analysis is compatible with the present theory, whereas that of Longobardi (1985) would not be, since in his analysis the postcopula phrase in (128) is higher than and yet to the right of VP. (A nonmovement analysis of the sort suggested by Ruwet (1982, chap. 6) would also be compatible.)

Moro's analysis raises a question about the formulation of note 57 that I will not pursue.

63. I agree here with Safir (1986, p. 665) on the general point that the two do not differ overtly, although the particular structure he assumes is not compatible with the present LCA-based theory.

64. Also see Keenan's (1985, p.169) more general point that overall the differences between restrictives and nonrestrictives are small.

65. Prenominal adjectives can have the structure '[D^0 [$_{CP}$ AP [C^0 [$_{IP}$ NP FP]]]], where AP has been moved to Spec,CP from within FP. In the nonrestrictive case AP will move up to Spec,DP at LF.

The commonality of nonrestrictive relatives and nonrestrictive adjectives is reinforced by the fact that both are incompatible with *the only;* that is, *the only industrious Greeks* cannot be nonrestrictive and (i) is not possible.

(i) *the only Greeks, who are industrious

66. Left open is the question of why, in English, French, and Italian, the intonation break precedes, rather than follows, the relative pronoun or complementizer.

67. The fact that IP-movement in Japanese can leave the relative to the right of an overt determiner/demonstrative implies that there must be at least two levels of D-like projection above CP.

Recall that, at least in the case where relativization is limited to subjects, there exists the possibility of moving a constituent smaller than IP to Spec,CP, as in (61).

68. Whether *these* originates in the embedded position with *pictures of himself* or instead is the upper D^0 whose sister is CP is a separate question that I will take up briefly in section 9.1.

Valentina Bianchi (personal communication) observes that counterparts of (134) are also possible in Italian. For example:

(i) Quella descrizione di se stesso, che Gianni ha letto nel   rapporto della
    that   description of himself   that Gianni has read in-the report   of-the
    polizia, è molto precisa.
    police is very   precise

Given (ii), there is a certain tension between Chomsky's reconstruction proposal and his (p. 21) discussion of the *easy to please*–construction.

(ii) Pictures of himself are hard for John to criticize.

69 It is unclear why (138) is less sharp with *lequel* 'the which'; see Kayne 1976, p. 270. For additional complexities in Italian, see Cinque 1978, 1982. Also unclear is why English nonrestrictives (unlike those of French and Italian) are not good with just a complementizer.

Cinque (1982, pp. 252, 260) takes the position that nonrestrictives can have the same structure as restrictives (a position with which I have agreed) but goes on to suggest that nonrestrictives can enter into a second, parenthetical structure (a position with which I have not agreed). Perhaps his arguments for a parenthetical structure can be reinterpreted in the spirit of the last paragraph of note 71. (Also perhaps relevant is whether IP in nonrestrictives can move farther leftward in LF, out of Spec,DP.)

70. Italian *cui* is not possible in free relatives, presumably for the same reason that it is not possible in interrogatives, unlike French *qui*. Thinking of the suggestion by Giuliana Giusti mentioned in note 12, it may be that *cui* requires spec-head agreement, whereas *qui*, like English *who*, is not so limited.

The very fact that *cui* is possible in nonrestrictives now argues that nonrestrictives are parallel to restrictives. See Nicolas Ruwet's comparable point concerning (138) noted by Emonds (1979, p. 230n.).

Emonds (p. 228) makes the interesting observation that a nonrestrictive relative does not license a postnominal adjective in English in the way that a complement does. This might be so because the relevant licensing takes place at LF, at a point after raising of the relative IP.

71. This would not be true in strongly head-final languages. The text analysis may therefore lead to an account of Emonds's (1979, p. 217n.) observation that Japanese allows recursion of nonrestrictives. This question needs to be pursued further.

Emonds further notes that Japanese lacks sentential nonrestrictives such as (i).

(i) John arrived late, which was unfortunate.

De Rijk (1972, p. 135) had conjectured that this is a general property of SOV languages. I would guess that it is more specifically a property of languages with only prenominal relatives.

Perhaps *John arrived late* in (i) is in Spec,*which*, so that the existence of (i) depends on the presence of a relative pronoun (or partially comparable element, like French *ce;* see Pollock 1992), which is not possible in prenominal relative structures, as discussed in section 8.3; also see (41) of chapter 7 and (43) and (54) of chapter 9.

72. Safir (1986, p. 673n.) mentions examples from a talk by Peter Sells that are exceptional with respect to (147), for reasons that are unclear.

Safir (p. 672) also mentions counterexamples to the apparent generalization that a pronoun within a nonrestrictive cannot be quantifier-bound from outside. Whether this phenomenon will turn out to be favorable or unfavorable to the text proposal is not clear, either. Note in this regard that, as Guéron (1980, n. 53) shows, even simple DPs can be opaque to such binding, with certain determiners.

Safir's (p. 673) observation that a nonrestrictive may not contain a parasitic gap bound from outside is not at present accounted for under my proposal. (One would like to know what the facts are concerning parasitic gaps and nonrestrictives in languages with prenominal relatives.)

Jackendoff (1977, p. 176) observes that the licensing of *any* cannot cross into a nonrestrictive. However, definite restrictives act similarly (see Fiengo and Higginbotham 1981; Fiengo 1987; May 1985, p. 145).

(i) *?I didn't see the man who had had any drinks.

(ii) *?John doesn't like the article that anybody mentioned.

73. Also see the discussion of (i) in Kayne 1985, p. 114.

(i) *They're trying to make advantage out to have been taken of them.

The reason for this property of idiom chunks remains to be made precise.

McCloskey (1979, p. 39) takes the existence of idiom chunk relatives with resumptive pronouns to constitute a problem for the raising/promotion analysis. Alternatively, in the spirit of section 7.3, such relatives could be taken to indicate that (in some languages) resumptive pronoun relatives result from the usual raising to Spec,CP, with the input being a clitic-doubling structure.

The present theory leads very definitely to the conclusion that resumptive pronoun relatives must be of the usual form, 'D^0 CP', with the "head" of the relative in Spec,CP. The LCA itself does not determine whether Spec,CP must be filled by movement or could perhaps be filled by "base generation." If movement is systematic, then new work on island constraints is called for.

It is not clear what to make of the rather artificial (ii), which is not possible as a restrictive.

(ii) this book, which masterpiece I have read twice, ...

Perhaps there is some link with Hindi correlatives (see Srivastav 1991); also see Keenan 1985, p. 152.

Chapter 9

1. See Baltin 1987, p. 585, and references cited there. Baltin's arguments for rightward movement based on antecedent-contained deletion are criticized by Larson and May (1990).

2. A base-generation approach of this sort is advocated by Rochemont and Culicover (1990) and for German by Wiltschko (1993). Also see Lasnik and Saito 1992, 104. Haider (1993) argues against right-adjunction, as I do, yet for base generation, as I do not.

3. Note that base generation (see note 2) would amount to treating them as free/headless relatives, making it difficult to understand why they resemble normal headed relatives and not free relatives, in a number of cases where headed and free relatives diverge.

For example, in English stranded relatives are like normal headed relatives and unlike free relatives in allowing *that*. Contrast (3) with (i).

(i) John ate what/*that Bill cooked.

In French stranded relatives are like normal headed relatives in disallowing direct object *qui* as a relative pronoun (see (15) and (138) of chapter 8).

(ii) *Quelqu'un est entré   qui je connais bien.
     someone   is entered who I know   well

Yet direct object *qui* is possible in free relatives; see (139) of chapter 8.

In Italian *cui* is possible in normal (see note 70 of chapter 8) and in stranded relatives (example from Cinque 1988, p. 472).

(iii) Ci   sono molte persone qui di cui   non ci possiamo fidare.
      there are   many people here of whom NEG us we-can   trust

But *cui* is impossible in free relatives.

(iv) *Cui non mangia non ingrassa.
      who NEG eats   NEG gets-fat

Possible instead of (iv) is (v) (example from Cinque 1988, p. 484).

(v) Chi non mangia non ingrassa.

But *chi*, which is also used in interrogatives, is impossible in both normal and stranded relatives.

There are thus many reasons from the domain of relative pronouns to take stranded relatives to be normal relatives that have been left behind upon movement of their "head."

4. A major difference between relatives and quantifiers concerns intermediate positions.

(i)   The men were all injured in the accident.

(ii)   *A man was who has no relatives injured in the accident.

It may be that the ungrammaticality of (ii) is an extreme case of the constraint against complex specifiers discussed earlier at (35) and (55) of chapter 8.

5. See the discussions of (14) and (58) of chapter 7, where the same point is made for heavy NP shift and right-dislocation.

6. The fact that there are two violations and in particular a theta-violation in (5) may account for the fact that (5) borders on the incomprehensible in a way that I think goes beyond even ECP violations.

7. See Huang's (1993, p. 115n.) argument against V'-fronting.

Leftward IP-movement that strands a zero complementizer is possible within DP in N-final languages; see the discussion of (41) of chapter 8. Whether such pre-D IPs can ever subsequently raise out of DP (and if not, why not) is left an open question.

To judge by Srivastav (1991), and in particular by her argument (p. 650) from multiple relativization, Hindi correlatives are not instances of ordinary relatives extracted from DP. Rather, as she notes (p. 680), they are somewhat like English free relatives, including those with *-ever* mentioned in note 13 of chapter 8.

8. Left open is the question of how to distinguish these cases from others where lack of a c-commanding antecedent seems not to lead to ungrammaticality; see the third paragraph of note 24 of chapter 8. Perhaps relevant is the focused status of *something* in (3), as discussed below in the text.

9. See Rochemont and Culicover 1990, p. 36, and references cited there. Rochemont and Culicover's account is based on right-adjunction and therefore incompatible with the present theory.

10. The constituent '[[e]$_i$ who ...]' following *up* in (14) is complement to *up*; see the discussion of particles in section 7.2.

11. VP-deletion can leave behind the relative in (i), as Baltin (1981, p. 267) observes.

(i) Although nobody would ride with Fred who knew just him, people would who knew his brother.

This cannot now be attributed to the relative being outside VP but must rather be assimilated to the phenomenon briefly discussed above at (26) of chapter 7, perhaps implying that the relative in (i) has moved above VP to the left (though remaining below its "head").

Note that (ii) is impossible, indicating clearly that it is asymmetric c-command rather than precedence that is at the heart of the matter.

(ii) *A man who had no money walked into any room.

Although (24) is marginally possible with *no* taking wide scope over *a*, it seems fully ungrammatical if interpreted with *a* having wide scope over *no*. This is probably related to the independent restriction on *any* mentioned at the end of note 72 of chapter 8.

12. With "free choice" *any* one might have (i).

(i) A man could walk into any room who had no money.

Here, of course, *any* is not being licensed by negation.

13. Many of these PPs may be reduced relatives in the extended sense of sections 8.4–8.6. I will not pursue PP-stranding further, however.

14. Contrary to Lasnik and Saito (1992, p. 100). Consider the fact that stranded PPs are sometimes compatible with extraction from within them.

(i) ?That's the house that I think I'm gonna send a photograph to John of the roof of.

15. From this perspective, *a man* is not itself a DP but is instead of some "smaller" category, perhaps QP. That is, Spec,IP in (33) is not filled by a full DP. This recalls Pesetsky's proposals (1982) about Russian and might lead to an understanding of why Italian has no relative clause stranding with preverbal subjects, as observed by Cinque (1982, n. 28). (The idea would be that Italian is like Russian in not allowing QP subjects; English and French would be different.)

In the same spirit, it might be that English (and Dutch/German) scrambling of the following sort is incompatible with QP.

(i) *John sent to someone a very valuable gift who he knows well.

Phrases with a demonstrative *the* as in (35) act like QP here.

(ii) *John sent to the very man a very valuable gift who he had just criticized.

If the subject position filled with QP in (33) and (35) counted as an A-position, then movement up to it from Spec,CP would produce an "improper movement" violation.

Improper movement from an Ā- to an A-position may underlie the impossibility of (iii), if derived by leftward movement of *a man who* from the Spec,CP whose associated IP is *we knew in high school*.

(iii) *A man who just walked in we knew in high school.

16. The fact that omitting *ever* does not improve (38) in the relevant reading suggests that free relatives without *ever* have some abstract counterpart to it. Perhaps also relevant here is the fact that QP cannot move past *the*, stranding it.

(i) *Man walked in the who I'd been telling her about.

Note that the analysis of *ever* as an outside D accounts for (ii).

(ii) *We'll hire the people whoever you choose.

The impossibility of (iii) can be attributed to the inability of a head to move into Spec,IP and/or to the inability of D to raise at all.

(iii) *Whatever came out late books I wanted to read.

17. Regarding the perhaps different case of stranding under *wh*-movement, Huot (1981, p. 268) has observed, however, that (in my terms) stranding of *de*-AP (see section 8.6) readily leaves *de*-AP in what looks like argument position in non-prepositional cases, but not in prepositional cases.

Perhaps relevant here is the fact that quantifier stranding under *wh*-movement is usually not possible with (nondative) prepositions; see Kayne 1975, secs. 1.2 and 2.14).

18. Pesetsky's (1995) idea that '... talk to John tomorrow' can correspond to a small clause structure embedded under *to* might be considered here, though it would not readily generalize to Dutch/German counterparts of (39).

19. Further movement of *someone* (= QP) by itself must be prohibited when P is lexical.

(i) *John is going to talk someone tomorrow to who he has a lot of faith in.

20. The left-adjoined *to* will c-command its trace, given the definition of c-command adopted earlier; see (16) of chapter 3.

To avoid the kind of violation discussed in section 3.7, it might suffice to say that a head X counts as being dominated by the category XP (its own maximal projection) even when moved to a position in which it is only included in XP. Thus, in (i)

(i) $[_{PP}[_{QP}$ to$_j$ $[_{QP}$ someone$_i]][_{PP}[e_j][_{DP}$ D $[_{CP}[e]_i \ldots$

to will count as being dominated by PP and hence will not c-command out of PP.

21. How to characterize "too deeply embedded" is an important question that is not central to the text discussion. (Chomsky (1981, p. 82, (9i)) accepts an example similar to (45) that I find unacceptable.)

22. Better than (47) for me with coreference is (i).

(i) He doesn't know what to do with it, John has so much money.

This construction might involve the preposing of the complement of the empty counterpart of result clause *that*.

23. On the clausal status of the object gap of *expected*, see Vergnaud 1975.

Chapter 10

1. Strictly speaking, it is the LCA plus the proposal given in sections 4.1–4.3 that together ensure the mapping to linear *precedence*.

2. The extra use of simultaneity available in sign languages like ASL raises an interesting question. Either hierarchical structure must be different there than in spoken language (if linear order really does not play the same role), or there must be a level of representation with greater linear ordering than is apparent that mediates between hierarchical structure and simultaneity.

For a very interesting application of the ideas of this monograph to questions of parsing, see Wu 1993.

3. Chomsky 1994 appeared too late to be discussed in this monograph.

4. Note that crossing branches of the sort advocated by McCawley (1982) are also excluded, given that asymmetric c-command implies precedence.

References

Ackema, P., A. Neeleman, and F. Weerman (1993). "Deriving Functional Projections." To appear in *Proceedings of NELS 23*.

Anderson, S. R. (1984). "Kwakwala Syntax and the Government-Binding Theory." In E.-D. Cook and D. B. Geerdts, eds., *The Syntax of Native American Languages*, 21–75. (Syntax and Semantics, vol. 16.) New York: Academic Press.

Anderson, S. R. (1992). *A-Morphous Morphology*. Cambridge: Cambridge University Press.

Antinucci, F., and G. Cinque (1977). "Sull'ordine delle parole in italiano: L'emarginazione." *Studi di grammatica italiana* 6, 121–146. (Reprinted in Cinque 1991.)

Aoun, J., and Y.-H. A. Li (1993). "*Wh*-Elements in Situ: Syntax or LF?" *Linguistic Inquiry* 24, 199–238.

Aoun, Y. [J. Aoun], and D. Sportiche (1981). "The Domain of Weak Cross-over Restrictions." In H. Borer and Y. Aoun, eds., *MIT Working Papers in Linguistics 3: Theoretical Issues in the Grammar of Semitic Languages*, 43–52. Department of Linguistics and Philosophy, MIT.

Azoulay-Vicente, A. (1985). *Les tours comportant l'expression* de + *adjectif*. Geneva: Droz.

Bach, E. (1971). "Questions." *Linguistic Inquiry* 2, 153–166.

Baker, M. C. (1988a). *Incorporation: A Theory of Grammatical Function Changing*. Chicago: University of Chicago Press.

Baker, M. C. (1988b). "Theta Theory and the Syntax of Applicatives in Chichewa," *Natural Language & Linguistic Theory* 6, 353–389.

Baltin, M. R. (1981). "Strict Bounding." In C. L. Baker and J. J. McCarthy, eds., *The Logical Problem of Language Acquisition*, 257–295. Cambridge, Mass.: MIT Press.

Baltin, M. R. (1987). "Do Antecedent-Contained Deletions Exist?" *Linguistic Inquiry* 18, 579–595.

Baltin, M. R. (1993). "Predicate Specifiers." Paper presented at the Graduate Center, City University of New York.

Bayer, J. (1984). "COMP in Bavarian Syntax." *The Linguistic Review* 3, 209–274.

Belletti, A. (1982). "On the Anaphoric Status of the Reciprocal Construction in Italian." *The Linguistic Review* 2, 101–137.

Belletti, A. (1990). *Generalized Verb Movement: Aspects of Verb Syntax.* Turin: Rosenberg and Sellier.

Belletti, A., and U. Shlonsky (to appear). "The Order of Verbal Complements: A Comparative Study." *Natural Language & Linguistic Theory.*

Benincà, P. (1988a). "Cenni sugli spostamenti a destra." In L. Renzi, ed., *Grande grammatica italiana di consultazione, vol. 1*, 145–148. Bologna: Il Mulino.

Benincà, P. (1988b). "Costruzioni con ordine marcato degli elementi." In L. Renzi ed., *Grande grammatica italiana di consultazione, vol. 1*, 129–143. Bologna: Il Mulino.

Benincà, P., and G. Cinque (1990). "On Certain Differences between Enclisis and Proclisis." Paper presented at the University of Geneva.

Benmamoun, E., and J.-R. Vergnaud (1994). "Directionality in Word Formation." Paper presented at the 17th GLOW Colloquium. *GLOW Newsletter* 32, 12–13.

Bernstein, J. B. (1993). "Topics in the Syntax of Nominal Structure across Romance." Doctoral dissertation, City University of New York.

Bhatt, R., and J. Yoon (1992). "On the Composition of COMP and Parameters of V2." In D. Bates, ed., *The Proceedings of the Tenth West Coast Conference on Formal Linguistics*, 41–52. Stanford, Calif.: CSLI Publications. (Distributed by the University of Chicago Press.)

Bittner, M., and K. Hale (1994). "The Structural Determination of Case." Ms., Rutgers University and MIT.

Bok-Bennema, R. (1994). "On the 'Syntactic' Properties of Morphology." Abstract, 17th GLOW Colloquium. *GLOW Newsletter* 32, 14–15.

Borer, H. (1989). "Anaphoric AGR." In O. Jaeggli and K. J. Safir, eds., *The Null Subject Parameter*, 69–109. Dordrecht: Kluwer.

Brame, M. K. (1976). *Conjectures and Refutations in Syntax and Semantics.* New York: North-Holland.

Brandon, F. R., and L. Seki (1981). "A Note on COMP as a Universal." *Linguistic Inquiry* 12, 659–665.

Branigan, P., and C. Collins (1993). "Verb Movement and the Quotative Construction in English." In J. D. Bobaljik and C. Phillips, eds., *MIT Working Papers in Linguistics 18: Papers on Case and Agreement 1*, 1–13. Department of Linguistics and Philosophy, MIT.

Bresnan, J. (1982). "The Passive in Lexical Theory." In J. Bresnan, ed., *The Mental Representation of Grammatical Relations*, 3–86. Cambridge, Mass.: MIT Press.

Bresnan, J., and J. Grimshaw (1978). "The Syntax of Free Relatives in English." *Linguistic Inquiry* 9, 331–391.

Brody, M. (1990). "Remarks on the Order of Elements in the Hungarian Focus Field." In I. Kenesei, ed., *Approaches to Hungarian*. Vol. 3: *Structures and Arguments*, 95–121. Jate Szeged.

Burridge, K. (1983). "On the Development of Dutch Negation." In H. Bennis and W. U. S. van Lessen Kloeke, eds., *Linguistics in the Netherlands 1983*, 31–40. Dordrecht: Foris.

Butz, B. (1981). *Morphosyntax der Mundart von Vermes (Val Terbi)*. Bern: Francke Verlag.

Cardinaletti, A. (1991). "On Pronoun Movement: The Italian Dative *Loro*." *Probus* 3, 127–153.

Cardinaletti, A., and I. Roberts (1990). "Levels of Representation of Agreement." Paper presented at the 13th GLOW Colloquium. *GLOW Newsletter* 24, 16–17.

Carlson, G. N. (1983). "Marking Constituents." In F. Heny and B. Richards, eds., *Linguistic Categories: Auxiliaries and Related Puzzles*. Vol. 1: *Categories*, 69–98. Dordrecht: Reidel.

Chiu, B. (1991). "*Suo*: An Object-Agreement in Mandarin Chinese." In S. Barbiers et al., eds., *LCJL3 Proceedings*, 77–95. University of Leiden.

Chomsky, N. (1957). *Syntactic Structures*. The Hague: Mouton.

Chomsky, N. (1973). "Conditions on Transformations." In S. R. Anderson and P. Kiparsky, eds., *A Festschrift for Morris Halle*, 232–286. New York: Holt, Rinehart and Winston.

Chomsky, N. (1976). "Conditions on Rules of Grammar." *Linguistic Analysis* 2, 303–351.

Chomsky, N. (1981). *Lectures on Government and Binding*. Dordrecht: Foris.

Chomsky, N. (1982). *Some Concepts and Consequences of the Theory of Government and Binding*. Cambridge, Mass.: MIT Press.

Chomsky, N. (1986a). *Barriers*. Cambridge, Mass.: MIT Press.

Chomsky, N. (1986b). *Knowledge of Language*. New York: Praeger.

Chomsky, N. (1991). "Some Notes on Economy of Derivation and Representation." In R. Freidin, ed., *Principles and Parameters in Comparative Grammar*, 417–454. Cambridge, Mass.: MIT Press.

Chomsky, N. (1993). "A Minimalist Program for Linguistic Theory." In K. Hale and S. J. Keyser, eds., *The View from Building 20: Essays in Linguistics in Honor of Sylvain Bromberger*, 1–52. Cambridge, Mass.: MIT Press.

Chomsky, N. (1994). "Bare Phrase Structure." *MIT Occasional Papers in Linguistics* 5. Department of Linguistics and Philosophy, MIT.

Chomsky, N., and H. Lasnik (1993). "Principles and Parameters Theory." In J. Jacobs, A. von Stechow, W. Sternefeld, and T. Vennemann, eds., *Syntax: An International Handbook of Contemporary Research*, 506–569. Berlin: Walter de Gruyter.

Chung, S., and J. McCloskey (1983). "On the Interpretation of Certain Island Facts in GPSG." *Linguistic Inquiry* 14, 704–713.

Cinque, G. (1977). "The Movement Nature of Left Dislocation." *Linguistic Inquiry* 8, 397–412.

Cinque, G. (1978). "La sintassi dei pronomi relativi *cui* e *quale* nell'italiano moderno." *Rivista di grammatica generativa* 3, 31–126. (Reprinted in Cinque 1991.)

Cinque, G. (1981). "On Keenan and Comrie's Primary Relativization Constraint." *Linguistic Inquiry* 12, 293–308.

Cinque, G. (1982). "On the Theory of Relative Clauses and Markedness." *The Linguistic Review* 1, 247–294.

Cinque, G. (1988). "La frase relativa." In L. Renzi, ed., *Grande grammatica italiana di consultazione, vol. 1*, 443–503. Bologna: Il Mulino.

Cinque, G. (1990). *Types of Ā-Dependencies*. Cambridge, Mass.: MIT Press.

Cinque, G. (1991). *Teoria linguistica e sintassi italiana*. Bologna: Il Mulino.

Cinque, G. (1992). "Functional Projections and N-Movement within the DP." Paper presented at the 15th GLOW Colloquium. *GLOW Newsletter* 28, 12–13.

Cinque, G. (1993a). "A Null Theory of Phrase and Compound Stress." *Linguistic Inquiry* 24, 239–297.

Cinque, G. (1993b). "On the Evidence for Partial N Movement in the Romance DP." Ms., University of Venice.

Cole, P. (1987). "The Structure of Internally Headed Relative Clauses." *Natural Language & Linguistic Theory* 5, 277–302.

Colombo, G. (1967). *Na bisa bòsa: Poesie in dialetto borgomanerese*. Borgomanero: Tinivella.

Cordin, P. (1990). "Visibilité du cas en Trentino." Paper presented at the First Workshop on the Syntax of Central Romance Languages, University of Geneva.

Cornilescu, A. (1992). "Remarks on the Determiner System of Rumanian: The Demonstratives *al* and *cel*." *Probus* 4, 189–260.

Coursaget-Colmerauer, C. (1975). "Etudes des structures du type nom de nom." Doctoral dissertation, University of Montreal.

Craig, C. (1977). *The Structure of Jacaltec*. Austin, Tex.: University of Texas Press.

Culioli, A. (1981). "Quelques problèmes de grammaire corse." In H. Geckeler et al., eds., *Logos Semantikos: Studia Linguistica in Honorem Eugenio Coseriu 1921–1981*, 161–172. Madrid: Gredos; Berlin: Walter de Gruyter.

de Rijk, R. P. G. (1972). "Relative Clauses in Basque: A Guided Tour." In P. M. Peranteau et al., eds., *The Chicago Which Hunt: Papers from the Relative Clause Festival*, 115–135. Chicago Linguistic Society, University of Chicago.

den Besten, H. (1977). "On the Interaction of Root Transformations and Lexical Deletive Rules." In W. Abraham, ed., *On the Formal Syntax of the Westgermania*, 47–131. Amsterdam: Benjamins.

den Besten, H., and G. Webelhuth (1990). "Stranding." In G. Grewendorf and W. Sternefeld, eds., *Scrambling and Barriers*, 77–92. Amsterdam: Academic Press.

den Dikken, M. (1992). "Particles." Dissertation, Holland Institute of Generative Linguistics.

Déprez, V. (1988). "Stylistic Inversion and Verb Movement." Ms., MIT.

Di Sciullo, A. M., and E. Williams (1987). *On the Definition of Word*. Cambridge, Mass.: MIT Press.

Dobrovie-Sorin, C. (1987). "A propos de la structure du groupe nominal en roumain." *Rivista di grammatica generativa* 12, 123–152.

Dobrovie-Sorin, C. (1990). "Clitic Doubling, *Wh*-Movement, and Quantification in Romanian." *Linguistic Inquiry* 21, 351–397.

Doherty, C. (to appear). "The Syntax of Subject Contact Relatives." In *Proceedings of CLS 29*.

Dougherty, R. C. (1971). "A Grammar of Coordinate Conjoined Structures: 2." *Language* 47, 298–339.

Downing, B. T. (1978). "Some Universals of Relative Clause Structure." In J. H. Greenberg, ed., *Universals of Human Language*. Vol. 4: *Syntax*, 375–418. Stanford, Calif.: Stanford University Press.

Duffield, N. (1994). "Are You Right? On Pronoun-Postposing and Other Problems of Irish Word Order." Paper presented at WCCFL 13, University of California, San Diego.

Emonds, J. (1976). *A Transformational Approach to English Syntax: Root, Structure-Preserving and Local Transformations*. New York: Academic Press.

Emonds, J. (1978). "The Verbal Complex V'-V in French." *Linguistic Inquiry* 9, 151–175.

Emonds, J. (1979). "Appositive Relatives Have No Properties." *Linguistic Inquiry* 10, 211–243.

Emonds, J. (1980). "Word Order in Generative Grammar." *Journal of Linguistic Research* 1, 33–54.

Everett, D. L. (1989). "Clitic Doubling, Reflexives, and Word Order Alternations in Yagua." *Language* 65, 339–372.

Fiengo, R. (1977). "On Trace Theory." *Linguistic Inquiry* 8, 35–61.

Fiengo, R. (1987). "Definiteness, Specificity and Familiarity." *Linguistic Inquiry* 18, 163–166.

Fiengo, R., and J. Higginbotham (1981). "Opacity in NP." *Linguistic Analysis* 7, 395–421.

Frampton, J. (1991). "Relativized Minimality: A Review." *The Linguistic Review* 8, 1–46.

Frank, R., Y.-S. Lee, and O. Rambow (1991). "Scrambling as Non-Operator Movement and the Special Status of Subjects." In S. Barbiers et al., eds., *LCJL3 Proceedings*, 135–154. University of Leiden.

Freeze, R. (1992). "Existentials and Other Locatives." *Language* 68, 553–595.

Fukui, N. (1986). "A Theory of Category Projection and Its Applications." Doctoral dissertation, MIT.

George, L. M., and J. Kornfilt (1981). "Finiteness and Boundedness in Turkish." In F. Heny, ed., *Binding and Filtering*, 105–127. London: Croom Helm.

Giacomo-Marcellesi, M. (1978). "La langue: Différentiations microrégionales et intercompréhension dans l'espace linguistique corse." In *Pieve e paesi: Communautés rurales corses*, 209–244. Paris: Editions du CNRS.

Giorgi, A., and G. Longobardi (1991). *The Syntax of Noun Phrases: Configuration, Parameters and Empty Categories*. Cambridge: Cambridge University Press.

Gleitman, L. R. (1969). "Coordinating Conjunctions in English." In D. A. Reibel and S. A. Schane, eds., *Modern Studies in English*, 80–112. Englewood Cliffs, N. J.: Prentice-Hall. (Reprinted from *Language* 41 (1965), 260–293.)

Godard, D. (1989). "Empty Categories as Subjects of Tensed Ss in English or French?" *Linguistic Inquiry* 20, 497–506.

Gragg, G. B. (1972). "Sumerian and Selected Afro-Asiatic Languages." In P. M. Peranteau et al., eds., *The Chicago Which Hunt: Papers from the Relative Clause Festival*, 153–168. Chicago Linguistic Society, University of Chicago.

Greenberg, J. H. (1966). "Some Universals of Grammar with Particular Reference to the Order of Meaningful Elements." In J. H. Greenberg, ed., *Universals of Language*, 73–113. 2nd ed. Cambridge, Mass.: MIT Press.

Groos, A., and H. van Riemsdijk (1981). "Matching Effects in Free Relatives: A Parameter of Core Grammar." In A. Belletti, L. Brandi, and L. Rizzi, eds., *Theory of Markedness in Generative Grammar: Proceedings of the 1979 GLOW Conference*, 171–216. Scuola Normale Superiore, Pisa.

Gross, M. (1968). *Grammaire transformationnelle du français: Syntaxe du verbe*. Paris: Larousse.

Gross, M. (1975). *Méthodes en syntaxe: Régime des constructions complétives*. Paris: Hermann.

Gross, M. (1977). *Grammaire transformationnelle du français: Syntaxe du nom*. Paris: Larousse.

Guéron, J. (1980). "On the Syntax and Semantics of PP Extraposition." *Linguistic Inquiry* 11, 637–678.

Guéron, J. (1987). "Clause Union and the Verb-Particle Construction in English." Paper presented at NELS 17.

Guéron, J., and R. May (1984). "Extraposition and Logical Form." *Linguistic Inquiry* 15, 1–31.

Haegeman, L. (1990). "Subject Pronouns and Subject Clitics in West-Flemish." *The Linguistic Review* 7, 333–363.

Haegeman, L. (1994). "The Typology of Agreement and the Dissociation of N- and V-related AGR." Abstract, 17th GLOW Colloquium. *GLOW Newsletter* 32, 26–27.

Haegeman, L., and R. Zanuttini (1991). "Negative Heads and the NEG Criterion." *The Linguistic Review*, 8, 233–251.

Haider, H. (1992). "Branching and Discharge." Ms., University of Stuttgart.

Haider, H. (1993). "Detached Clauses: The Later the Deeper." Ms., University of Stuttgart.

Hale, K., and S. J. Keyser (1993). "On Argument Structure and the Lexical Expression of Syntactic Relations." In K. Hale and S. J. Keyser, eds., *The View from Building 20: Essays in Linguistics in Honor of Sylvain Bromberger*, 53–109. Cambridge, Mass.: MIT Press.

Harbert, W., and V. Srivastav (1988). "A Complement/Adjunct Binding Asymmetry in Hindi and Other Languages." In *Cornell Working Papers in Linguistics* 8, 79–105. Department of Linguistics, Cornell University.

Heim, I., H. Lasnik, and R. May (1991). "Reciprocity and Plurality." *Linguistic Inquiry*. 22, 63–101.

Hermon, G. (1985). *Syntactic Modularity*. Dordrecht: Foris.

Hestvik, A. (1992). "LF Movement of Pronouns and Antisubject Orientation." *Linguistic Inquiry* 23, 557–594.

Hirschbühler, P. (1975). "On the Source of Lefthand NPs in French." *Linguistic Inquiry* 6, 155–165.

Hirschbühler, P., and M.-L. Rivero (1983). "Remarks on Free Relatives and Matching Phenomena." *Linguistic Inquiry* 14, 505–520.

Hirst, D. (1993). "Detaching Intonational Phrases from Syntactic Structure." *Linguistic Inquiry* 24, 781–788.

Hoji, H. (1994). "Null Object Construction and Sloppy Identity in Japanese." (Abstract of) paper presented at the Formal Approaches to Japanese Linguistics conference, MIT.

Holmberg, A., and C. Platzack (to appear). *The Role of Inflection in Scandinavian Syntax*. Oxford: Oxford University Press.

Hornstein, N. (1994). "An Argument for Minimalism: The Case of Antecedent-Contained Deletion." *Linguistic Inquiry* 25, 455–480.

Huang, C. T. J. (1982). "Logical Relations in Chinese and the Theory of Grammar." Doctoral dissertation, MIT.

Huang, C.-T. J. (1993). "Reconstruction and the Structure of VP: Some Theoretical Consequences." *Linguistic Inquiry* 24, 103–138.

Huang, C.-T. J., and C.-C. J. Tang (1991). "The Local Nature of the Long-Distance Reflexive in Chinese." In J. Koster and E. Reuland, eds., *Long-Distance Anaphora*, 263–282. Cambridge: Cambridge University Press.

Huot, H. (1981). *Constructions infinitives du français: Le subordonnant* de. Geneva-Paris: Droz.

Iatridou, S. (1991). "Clitics and Island Effects." Ms., MIT.

Jackendoff, R. (1977). $\bar{X}$ *Syntax: A Study of Phrase Structure.* Cambridge, Mass.: MIT Press.

Jaeggli, O. A. (1986). "Three Issues in the Theory of Clitics: Case, Doubled NPs, and Extraction." In H. Borer, ed., *The Syntax of Pronominal Clitics,* 15–42. (Syntax and Semantics, vol. 19.) Orlando, Fla.: Academic Press.

Jayaseelan, K. A. (1985). "Incomplete Deletion of VP's, Compared Constituents and Clauses." Ms., Central Institute of English and Foreign Languages, Hyderabad (India).

Jayaseelan, K. A. (1991). "The Pronominal System of Malayalam." In *CIEFL Occasional Papers in Linguistics* (Hyderabad) 3, 68–107.

Jespersen, O. (1974 (1927)). *A Modern English Grammar on Historical Principles.* Part 3: *Syntax (Second Volume).* London: George Allen & Unwin, and Copenhagen: Ejnar Munksgaard.

Johnson, K. (1991). "Object Positions." *Natural Language & Linguistic Theory* 9, 577–636.

Kayne, R. S. (1975). *French Syntax: The Transformational Cycle.* Cambridge, Mass.: MIT Press.

Kayne, R. S. (1976). "French Relative 'que'." In F. Hensey and M. Luján, eds., *Current Studies in Romance Linguistics,* 255–299. Washington, D.C.: Georgetown University Press.

Kayne, R. S. (1980). "Extensions of Binding and Case-Marking." *Linguistic Inquiry* 11, 75–96. (Reprinted in Kayne 1984.)

Kayne, R. S. (1981a). "ECP Extensions." *Linguistic Inquiry* 12, 93–133. (Reprinted in Kayne 1984.)

Kayne, R. S. (1981b). "On Certain Differences between French and English." *Linguistic Inquiry* 12, 349–371. (Reprinted in Kayne 1984.)

Kayne, R. S. (1981c). "Unambiguous Paths." In R. May and J. Koster, eds., *Levels of Syntactic Representation,* 143–183. Dordrecht: Foris. (Reprinted in Kayne 1984.)

Kayne, R. S. (1983a). "Chains, Categories External to S and French Complex Inversion." *Natural Language & Linguistic Theory* 1, 107–139 (Reprinted in Kayne 1984.)

Kayne, R. S. (1983b). "Connectedness." *Linguistic Inquiry* 14, 223–249 (Reprinted in Kayne 1984.)

Kayne, R. S. (1984). *Connectedness and Binary Branching.* Dordrecht: Foris.

Kayne, R. S. (1985). "Principles of Particle Constructions." In J. Guéron, H.-G. Obenauer, and J.-Y. Pollock, eds., *Grammatical Representation, 101–140.* Dordrecht: Foris.

Kayne, R. S. (1986). "Connexité et inversion du sujet." in M. Ronat and D. Couquaux, eds., *La grammaire modulaire,* 127–147. Paris: Editions de Minuit.

Kayne, R. S. (1989a). "Notes on English Agreement." *CIEFL Bulletin* 1, 41–67.

Kayne, R. S. (1989b). "Null Subjects and Clitic Climbing." In O. Jaeggli and K. J. Safir, eds., *The Null Subject Parameter*, 239–261. Dordrecht: Kluwer.

Kayne, R. S. (1991). "Romance Clitics, Verb Movement, and PRO." *Linguistic Inquiry* 22, 647–686.

Kayne, R. S. (1993). "Toward a Modular Theory of Auxiliary Selection." *Studia Linguistica* 47, 3–31.

Keenan, E. L. (1985). "Relative Clauses." In T. Shopen, ed., *Language Typology and Syntactic Description*. Vol. 2: *Complex Constructions*, 141–170. Cambridge: Cambridge University Press.

Koizumi, M. (1993). "Object Agreement Phrases and the Split VP Hypothesis." In J. D. Bobaljik and C. Phillips, eds., *MIT Working Papers in Linguistics 18: Papers on Case and Agreement 1*, 99–148. Department of Linguistics and Philosophy, MIT.

Koopman, H. (1984). *The Syntax of Verbs: From Verb Movement Rules in the Kru Languages to Universal Grammar*. Dordrecht: Foris.

Koopman, H. (1993a). "The Internal and External Distribution of Pronominal DPs." Ms., UCLA.

Koopman, H. (1993b). "The Structure of Dutch PPs." Ms., UCLA.

Koster, J. (1987). *Domains and Dynasties: The Radical Autonomy of Syntax*. Dordrecht: Foris.

Koster, J. (1993). "Predicate Incorporation and the Word Order of Dutch." Ms., University of Groningen.

Krishnamurti, Bh., and J. P. L. Gwynn (1985). *A Grammar of Modern Telugu*. Delhi: Oxford University Press.

Kuno, S. (1973). *The Structure of the Japanese Language*. Cambridge, Mass.: MIT Press.

Kuno, S. (1975). "Conditions for Verb Phrase Deletion." *Foundations of Language* 13, 161–175.

Kuno, S. (1976). "Gapping: A Functional Analysis." *Linguistic Inquiry* 7, 300–318.

Kupferman, L. (1991). "Structure événementielle de l'alternance *un/∅* devant les noms humains attributs." *Langages* 102, 52–75.

Kupferman. L. (to appear). "Une assignation de Cas assez exceptionnelle." *Lingvisticae Investigationes*.

Kuroda, S.-Y. (1988). "Whether We Agree or Not: A Comparative Syntax of English and Japanese." *Lingvisticae Investigationes* 12, 1–47.

Laka, I. (1990). "Negation in Syntax: On the Nature of Functional Categories and Projections." Doctoral dissertation, MIT.

Laka, I. (1993). "Unergative That Assign Ergative, Unaccusatives That Assign Accusative." In J. D. Bobaljik and C. Phillips, eds., *MIT Working Papers in Linguistics 18: Papers on Case and Agreement 1*, 149–172. Department of Linguistics and Philosophy, MIT.

Lakoff, G., and S. Peters (1969). "Phrasal Conjunction and Symmetric Predicates." In D. A. Reibel and S. A. Schane, eds., *Modern Studies in English*. 113–142. Englewood Cliffs, N.J.: Prentice-Hall.

Larson, R. K. (1987). "'Missing Prepositions' and the Analysis of English Free Relative Clauses." *Linguistic Inquiry* 18, 239–266.

Larson, R. K. (1988). "On the Double Object Construction." *Linguistic Inquiry* 19, 335–391.

Larson, R. K. (1990). "Double Objects Revisited: Reply to Jackendoff." *Linguistic Inquiry* 21, 589–632.

Larson, R. K., and R. May (1990). "Antecedent Containment or Vacuous Movement: Reply to Baltin." *Linguistic Inquiry* 21, 103–122.

Lasnik, H., and. M. Saito (1992). *Move α: Conditions on Its Application and Output*. Cambridge, Mass.: MIT Press.

Law, P. (1991). "Verb Movement, Expletive Replacement, and Head Government." *The Linguistic Review* 8, 253–285.

Levine, R. D. (1985). "Right Node (Non-)Raising." *Linguistic Inquiry* 16, 492–497.

Li, C. N., and S. A. Thompson (1981). *Mandarin Chinese: A Functional Reference Grammar*. Berkeley, Calif.: University of California Press.

Longobardi, G. (1985). "Su alcune proprietà della sintassi e della forma logica delle frasi copulari." In L. M. Savoia and A. Franchi de Bellis, eds., *Sintassi e morfologia della lingua italiana d'uso*, 211–223. Rome: Bulzoni.

Longobardi, G. (1992). "In Defense of the Correspondence Hypothesis: Island Effects and Parasitic Constructions in Logical Form." In C.-T. J. Huang and R. May, eds., *Logical Structure and Linguistic Structure: Cross-Linguistic Perspectives*, 149–196. Dordrecht: Kluwer.

Longobardi, G. (to appear). "Reference and Proper Names: A Theory of N-movement in Syntax and Logical Form." *Linguistic Inquiry*.

Marácz, L. (1989). "Asymmetries in Hungarian." Doctoral dissertation, University of Groningen.

Marantz, A. (1984). *On the Nature of Grammatical Relations*. Cambridge, Mass.: MIT Press.

May, R. (1985). *Logical Form*. Cambridge, Mass.: MIT Press.

McCawley, J. (1982). "Parentheticals and Discontinuous Constituent Structure." *Linguistic Inquiry* 13, 91–106.

McCloskey, J. (1979). *Transformational Syntax and Model Theoretic Semantics: A Case Study in Modern Irish*. Dordrecht: D. Reidel.

McCloskey, J. (1986). "Right Node Raising and Preposition Stranding." *Linguistic Inquiry* 17, 183–186.

McCloskey, J. (1992). "On the Scope of Verb Movement in Irish." Ms., University of California, Santa Cruz.

McCloskey, J., and K. Hale (1984). "On the Syntax of Person-Number Inflection in Modern Irish." *Natural Language & Linguistic Theory* 1, 487–533.

Milner, J.-C. (1978). *De la syntaxe à l'interprétation. Quantités, insultes, exclamations*. Paris: Editions du Seuil.

Moro, A. (1991). "The Raising of Predicates: Copula, Expletives and Existence." In L. L. S. Cheng and H. Demirdash, eds., *MIT Working Papers in Linguistics 15: More papers on Wh-Movement*, 183–218. Department of Linguistics and Philosophy, MIT.

Moro, A. (1993). *I predicati nominali e la struttura della frase*. Padua: Unipress.

Mosel, U., and E. Hovdhaugen (1992). *Samoan Reference Grammar*. Oslo: Scandinavian University Press, The Institute for Comparative Research in Human Culture.

Mouchaweh, L. (1985). "De la quantification à distance et des nominalisations en français." *Modèles linguistiques* 7, 91–117.

Mulder, R. (1992). "The Aspectual Nature of Syntactic Complementation." Dissertation, Holland Institute of Generative Linguistics.

Müller, G. (1994). "A Constraint on Remnant Movement." Paper presented at the 9th Comparative Germanic Syntax Workshop, Harvard University.

Munn, A. (1992). "A Null Operator Analysis of ATB Gaps." *The Linguistic Review* 9, 1–26.

Munn, A. (1993). "Topics in the Syntax and Semantics of Coordinate Structures." Doctoral dissertation, University of Maryland.

Muysken, P. (1982). "Parametrizing the Notion 'Head.'" *Journal of Linguistic Research* 2, 57–75.

Napoli, D. J. (1989). *Predication Theory: A Case Study for Indexing Theory*. Cambridge: Cambridge University Press.

Nkemnji, M. A. (1992). "Issues in the Syntax of Negation in Nweh." Master's thesis, UCLA.

Obenauer, H.-G. (1976). *Etudes de syntaxe interrogative du français*: Quoi, combien *et le complémenteur*. Tübingen: Max Niemeyer.

Ordóñez Lao, F. (1994). "Postverbal Asymmetries in Spanish." Paper presented at the 17th GLOW Colloquium. *GLOW Newsletter* 32, 40–41.

O Siadhail, M. (1989). *Modern Irish: Grammatical Structure and Dialectal Variation*. Cambridge: Cambridge University Press.

Otani, K., and J. Whitman (1991). "V-Raising and VP-Ellipsis." *Linguistic Inquiry* 22, 345–358.

Parry, M. (1984). "The Dialect of Cairo Montenotte." Doctoral dissertation, University of Wales, Aberystwyth.

Payne, J. R. (1985). "Complex Phrases and Complex Sentences." In T. Shopen, ed., *Language Typology and Syntactic Description*. Vol. 2: *Complex Constructions*, 3–41. Cambridge: Cambridge University Press.

Perlmutter, D. M. (1970). "On the Article in English." In M. Bierwisch and K. E. Heidolph, eds., *Progress in Linguistics*, 233–248. The Hague: Mouton.

Pesetsky, D. (1982). "Paths and Categories." Doctoral dissertation, MIT.

Pesetsky, D. (1995). *Zero Syntax: Experiencers and Cascades*. Cambridge, Mass.: MIT Press.

Pica, P. (1987). "On the Nature of the Reflexivization Cycle." In J. McDonough and B. Plunkett, eds., *Proceedings of NELS 17*, 483–499. GLSA, University of Massachusetts, Amherst.

Platzack, C. (1985). "The Position of the Finite Verb in Swedish." in H. Haider and M. Prinzhorn, eds., *Verb Second Phenomena in Germanic Languages*, 27–47. Dordrecht: Foris.

Platzack, C. (1992). "ϕ-Features as Clitics." Ms., University of Lund.

Poletto, C. (1992). "La sintassi del soggetto nei dialetti italiani settentrionali." Doctoral dissertation, University of Padua.

Pollock, J.-Y. (1983). "Sur quelques propriétés des phrases copulatives en français, *Langue française* 58, 89–125.

Pollock, J.-Y. (1985). "On Case and the Syntax of Infinitives in French." In J. Guéron, H.-G. Obenauer, and J.-Y. Pollock, eds. *Grammatical Representation*, 293–326. Dordrecht: Foris.

Pollock, J.-Y. (1989). "Verb Movement, Universal Grammar, and the Structure of IP." *Linguistic Inquiry* 20, 365–424.

Pollock, J.-Y. (1992). "Opérateurs nuls, *dont*, questions indirectes, et théorie de la quantification." In L. Tasmowski and A. Zribi-Hertz, eds., *Hommages à Nicolas Ruwet*, 440–463. Ghent: Communication & Cognition.

Postal, P. M. (1974). *On Raising: One Rule of English Grammar and Its Theoretical Implications*. Cambridge, Mass.: MIT Press.

Postal, P. M. (1990). "French Indirect Object Demotion." In P. M. Postal and B. D. Joseph, eds., *Studies in Relational Grammar 3*, 104–200. Chicago: University of Chicago Press.

Postal, P. M. (1993). "Parasitic Gaps and the Across-the-Board Phenomenon." *Linguistic Inquiry* 24, 735–754.

Postal, P. M. (n.d.). "Right Node Raising and Extraction." Ms., New York.

Raposo, E. (1987). "Romance Infinitival Clauses and Case Theory." In C. Neidle and R. Nuñez-Cedeño, eds., *Studies in Romance Languages*, 237–249. Dordrecht: Foris.

Reinhart, T. (1983). *Anaphora and Semantic Interpretation*, London: Croom Helm.

Remacle, L. (1952). *Syntaxe du parler wallon de La Gleize*. Tome 1: *Noms et articles—Adjectifs et pronoms*. Paris: Les Belles Lettres.

Riemsdijk, H. van (1978). *A Case Study in Syntactic Markedness*. Lisse: The Peter de Ridder Press.

Riemsdijk, H. van (1989). "Movement and Regeneration." In P. Benincà, ed., *Dialect Variation and the Theory of Grammar. 105–136.* Dordrecht: Foris.

Rivero, M.-L. (1994). "Clause Structure and V-Movement in the Languages of the Balkans." *Natural Language & Linguistic Theory* 12, 63–120.

Rivero, M.-L. (to appear). "Negation, Imperatives, and Wackernagel Effects." *Rivista di linguistica.*

Rizzi, L. (1982). *Issues in Italian Syntax.* Dordrecht: Foris.

Rizzi, L. (1990a). "On the Anaphor-Agreement Effect." *Rivista di linguistica* 2, 27–42.

Rizzi, L. (1990b). *Relativized Minimality.* Cambridge, Mass.: MIT Press.

Rizzi, L. (1991). "Residual Verb Second and the Wh Criterion." Ms., University of Geneva.

Rizzi, L., and I. Roberts (1989). "Complex Inversion in French." *Probus* 1, 1–30.

Roberts, I. (1991). "Excorporation and Minimality." *Linguistic Inquiry* 22, 209–218.

Roberts, I., and U. Shlonsky (1994). "Pronominal Enclisis in VSO Languages." Paper presented at the 17th GLOW Colloquium. *GLOW Newsletter* 32, 50–51.

Rochemont, M. S., and P. W. Culicover (1990). *English Focus Constructions and the Theory of Grammar.* Cambridge: Cambridge University Press.

Ronat, M. (1977). "Une contrainte sur l'effacement du nom." In M. Ronat, ed., *Langue: Théorie générative étendue,* 153–169. Paris: Hermann.

Ronat, M. (1979). "Pronoms topiques et pronoms distinctifs." *Langue française* 44, 106–128.

Ronat, M. (1982). "Logical Form and Prosodic Islands." *Journal of Linguistic Research* 2, 33–48.

Ronat, M. (1984). "Le liage prosodique: L'intonation comme anaphore." In J.-C. Milner, ed., *Recherches sur l'anaphore,* 13–34. University of Paris 7.

Rooryck, J. (1992). "Romance Enclitic Ordering and Universal Grammar." To appear in *The Linguistic Review.*

Ross, J. R. (1967). "Constraints on Variables in Syntax." Doctoral dissertation, MIT.

Rouveret, A. (1978). "Result Clauses and Conditions on Rules." In S. J. Keyser, ed., *Recent Transformational Studies in European Languages,* 159–187. Cambridge, Mass.: MIT Press.

Ruwet, N. (1982). *Grammaire des insultes et autres études.* Paris: Editions du Seuil.

Safir, K. (1986). "Relative Clauses in a Theory of Binding and Levels." *Linguistic Inquiry* 17, 663–689.

Savio, S. D. (1991). "Wh-Questions in Tamil." In *CIEFL Occasional Papers in Linguistics* (Hyderabad) 3, 55–67.

Schachter, P. (1973). "Focus and Relativization." *Language* 49, 19–46.

Schachter, P., and F. T. Otanes (1972). *Tagalog Reference Grammar*. Berkeley, Calif.: University of California Press.

Shlonsky, U. (1994). "Semitic Clitics." Paper presented at the LSA conference, Boston.

Smith, C. S. (1969). "Determiners and Relative Clauses in a Generative Grammar of English." In D. A. Reibel and S. A. Schane, eds., *Modern Studies in English*, 247–263. Englewood Cliffs, N.J.: Prentice-Hall. (Reprinted from *Language* 40 (1964), 37–52.)

Sobin, N. (1987). "The Variable Status of Comp-Trace Phenomena." *Natural Language & Linguistic Theory* 5, 33–60.

Sportiche, D. (1988). "A Theory of Floating Quantifiers and Its Corollaries for Constituent Structure." *Linguistic Inquiry* 19, 425–449.

Sportiche, D. (1992). "Clitics, Voice and Spec/Head Licensing." Paper presented at the 15th GLOW Colloquium. *GLOW Newsletter* 28, 46–47.

Sportiche, D. (n.d.). "Subject Clitics in French and Romance: Complex Inversion and Clitic Doubling." Ms., UCLA.

Srivastav, V. (1991). "The Syntax and Semantics of Correlatives." *Natural Language & Linguistic Theory* 9, 637–686.

Steever, S. B. (1987). "Tamil and the Dravidian Languages." In B. Comrie, ed., *The World's Major Languages*, 725–746. New York: Oxford University Press.

Stowell, T. A. (1981). "Origins of Phrase Structure." Doctoral dissertation, MIT.

Szabolcsi, A. (1981). "The Possessive Construction in Hungarian: A Configurational Category in a Non-Configurational Language." *Acta Linguistica Academiae Scientiarum Hungaricae* 31, 261–289.

Szabolcsi, A. (1983). "The Possessor That Ran Away from Home." *The Linguistic Review* 3, 89–102.

Szabolcsi, A. (1992). "Subordination: Articles and Complementizers." In I. Kenesei and C. Pléh, eds., *Approaches to Hungarian*. Vol. 4: *The Structure of Hungarian*, 123–137. Jate Szeged.

Szabolcsi, A. (to appear). "The Noun Phrase." In F. Kiefer and K. É. Kiss, eds., *The Syntactic Structure of Hungarian*. San Diego, Calif.: Academic Press.

Taraldsen, K. T. (1978). "The Scope of *Wh* Movement in Norwegian." *Linguistic Inquiry* 9, 624–640.

Taraldsen, K. T. (1981). "The Theoretical Interpretation of a Class of 'Marked' Extractions." In A. Belletti, L. Brandi, and L. Rizzi, eds., *Theory of Markedness in Generative Grammar: Proceedings of the 1979 GLOW Conference*, 475–516. Scuola Normale Superiore, Pisa.

Thiersch, C. (1993). "On the Formal Properties of Constituent Coordination." Paper presented at the 16th GLOW Colloquium. *GLOW Newsletter* 30, 70–71.

Thráinsson, H. (1985). "V1, V2, V3 in Icelandic." In H. Haider and M. Prinzhorn, eds., *Verb Second Phenomena in Germanic Languages*, 169–194. Dordrecht: Foris.

Torrego, E. (1983). "More Effects of Successive Cyclic Movement." *Linguistic Inquiry* 14, 561–565.

Travis, L. (1989). "Parameters of Phrase Structure." In A. S. Kroch and M. R. Baltin, eds., *Alternative Conceptions of Phrase Structure*, 263–279. Chicago: University of Chicago Press.

Tuller, L. (1992). "Postverbal Focus Constructions in Chadic." *Natural Language & Linguistic Theory* 10, 303–334.

Ultan, R. (1978). "Some General Characteristics of Interrogative Systems." In J. H. Greenberg, ed., *Universals of Human Language*. Vol. 4: *Syntax*, 211–248. Stanford, Calif.: Stanford University Press.

Uriagereka, J. (1988). "On Government." Doctoral dissertation, University of Connecticut.

Uriagereka, J. (n.d.). "Some Issues on Clitic Placement in Western Romance." Ms., University of Maryland.

Uriagereka, J. (to appear). "An F Position in Western Romance." In K. É. Kiss, ed., *Discourse Configurational Languages*. New York: Oxford University Press.

Vergnaud, J.-R. (1974). "French Relative Clauses." Doctoral dissertation, MIT. (Revised version in Vergnaud 1985.)

Vergnaud, J.-R. (1975). "La réduction du noeud S dans les relatives et les comparatives." *Rapport de Recherches, Laboratoire d'Automatique Documentaire et Linguistique*, University of Paris 7 and University of Paris 8.

Vergnaud, J.-R. (1985). *Dépendances et niveaux de représentation en syntaxe*. Amsterdam: John Benjamins.

Vinet, M.-T. (1977). "Etudes sur le syntagme nominal: La dislocation, l'adjectif 'propre.'" Thèse de doctorat de troisième cycle, University of Paris 8.

Wali, K., and K. V. Subbarao (1991). "On Pronominal Classification: Evidence from Marathi and Telugu." *Linguistics* 29, 1093–1110.

Webelhuth, G. (1992). *Principles and Parameters of Syntactic Saturation*. New York: Oxford University Press.

Wexler, K., and P. W. Culicover (1980). *Formal Principles of Language Acquisition*. Cambridge, Mass.: MIT Press.

Whitman, J. (1994). "Rightward Head Movement." Abstract, Formal Approaches to Japanese Linguistics conference, MIT.

Williams, E. S. (1975). "Small Clauses in English." In J. P. Kimball, ed., *Syntax and Semantics, Volume 4*, 249–273. New York: Academic Press.

Williams, E. S. (1977), "Discourse and Logical Form." *Linguistic Inquiry* 8, 101–139.

Williams, E. S. (1981). "On the Notions 'Lexically Related' and 'Head of a Word,'" *Linguistic Inquiry* 12, 245–274.

Williams, E. (1990). "The ATB Theory of Parasitic Gaps." *The Linguistic Review* 6, 265–279.

Williamson, J. S. (1987). "An Indefiniteness Restriction for Relative Clauses in Lakhota." In J. Koster and E. Reuland, eds., *Long-Distance Anaphora* 168–190. Cambridge: Cambridge University Press.

Wiltschko, M. (1993). "Extraposition in German. "Ms., University of Vienna.

Wu, A. (1993). "The S-Parameter." Paper presented at the 16th GLOW Colloquium. *GLOW Newsletter* 30, 60–61.

Yadurajan, K. S. (1988). "Binding Theory and Reflexives in Dravidian." In *Cornell Working Papers in Linguistics* 8, 181–203. Department of Linguistics, Cornell University.

Yvia Croce, H. (1979). *Grammaire corse.* Ajaccio: Editions Cyrnos et Méditerranée.

Zanuttini, R. (to appear). "Speculations on Negative Imperatives." *Rivista di linguistica.*

Ziv, Y., and P. Cole (1974). "Relative Extraposition and the Scope of Definite Descriptions in Hebrew and English." In M. W. La Galy et al., eds., *Papers from the Tenth Regional Meeting. Chicago Linguistic Society,* 772–786. Chicago Linguistic Society, University of Chicago.

Zwart, C. J. W. (1993). "Dutch Syntax: A Minimalist Approach." Doctoral dissertation, University of Groningen.

Zwart, C. J. W. (to appear). "Dutch Is Head-Initial." *The Linguistic Review.*

Index